BURMA AND BEYOND

BURMA AND BEYOND

The true story of a family devastated by war

Maude Kilvington

To: Celia + John,
with best wishes,
Maude Kilvington.

17th Oct. 2010.

Crosswave
Publishing

First published in 2010

Crosswave Publishing
1 Victoria Road
Chichester
West Sussex
PO19 7HY

ISBN 978-0-9565561-1-0

© Maude Kilvington, 2010

Maps by Tim Aspden

Set in Sylfaen and Albertus Extra Bold

Printed in Great Britain by Imprint Digital (imprintdigital.net)

In loving memory of
my brother Richard
to whom I owe my days

Family Tree

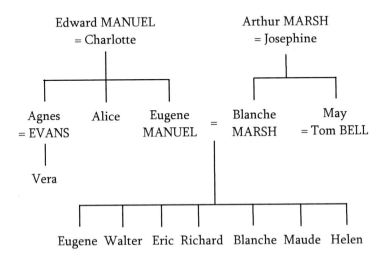

Edward MANUEL = Charlotte

Arthur MARSH = Josephine

Agnes = EVANS

Alice

Eugene MANUEL =

Blanche MARSH

May = Tom BELL

Vera

Eugene Walter Eric Richard Blanche Maude Helen

Contents

Acknowledgements

Many people have helped and encouraged me in the writing and presentation of this record of my early life. My thanks go first of all to my friends in Spain, who could not wait for the next chapter to be written as I tried to resurrect buried memories, and to my family who initially did not wish to be reminded of the horrors of those times but later relented and without whose contribution I could not have told the full story. And later, much later, my church family who wondered if it would be finished at all. I thank Roger Yardley, Elisabeth Thompson and Tracey Hills for 'tweaking' my work here and there, and especially Adrian Higham for his advice and help in sorting out the many strands of the story into some semblance of order. Finally, I thank Jeff Vinter for spending hours at his computer in the final editing, scanning of photographs and preparation of this book for publication. To all these good people of St. George's Church, Whyke, Chichester, my heartfelt and sincere thanks.

All the photographs were taken by members of my family except for that on page 80, the source of which is unknown. If any reader can provide an attribution, the publisher will be pleased to make the necessary arrangements.

Prologue

I had never intended writing about my early life. The events that took place in my youth were over, almost forgotten, in the dark recesses of my mind.

Now, in the autumn of my life, surrounded by new friends, I felt relaxed and happy. Here we were at the home of Verlan and Carlos to celebrate Thanksgiving Day. Fourteen of us were gathered round the table, having just enjoyed a delicious lunch of turkey and cranberry sauce with all the trimmings, and pumpkin pie to follow. The wine flowed freely; the atmosphere friendly and relaxed. We were all enjoying the pleasantries of the evening, laughing at jokes being retold for the twentieth time, when the conversation switched to stories of our past lives and how we came to be gathered here together in captivating Cataluña – all from different countries and backgrounds. Our host, Verlan, was from Bakersfield, USA, and his partner, Carlos, from Madrid and this, their lovely villa, overlooked the clear blue waters that formed the Bay of Rosas.

It was Peter, my brother-in-law, who suddenly interrupted the conversation by saying loudly; "You haven't heard Maude's story, have you? What an amazing life she's led! Do you know she walked miles through the jungle trying to escape the Japanese in Burma!"

I was a bit taken aback at this sudden remark, for I had almost forgotten the events of those far off days. They were too painful to recall. Had I not been trying, for fifty or more years, to forget them? They were gone, in the past. But Mary said, "Burma? What's your connection with Burma? Where is it? How did you come to be involved in the war with Japan? Do tell us your story, Maude, we'd love to know about Burma."

Mary's home is in Montana, USA. She is well read and well travelled but had never heard of Burma. René and Carla, Anneké and Johan also persisted, urging me on. They all wanted to hear my story.

And so it was that I started to tell of my family, our idyllic life in India, our move to Burma. Then of the disaster that befell the family when Japanese forces invaded the country in 1942 and the final sad days of my mother's life. When I came to the part of my story relating to my mother I felt I could not go on. Josè was so concerned about me in the telling that she lost the thread of the story. She fetched me a glass of water. Albert squeezed my hand reassuringly. The group fell silent. Sad. The laughter had ceased.

Roy said, "That's quite a story, Maude, quite unbelievable. You should write it down. Most people here don't know much about what happened on the other side of the world during the war. Besides, your children and grandchildren will need to know what you went through."

"I wouldn't know where to start."

"Start with your earliest memories, Maude, before

you went to Burma." said Meiké, from Amsterdam, "You must start writing. It is part of your history, part of our history."

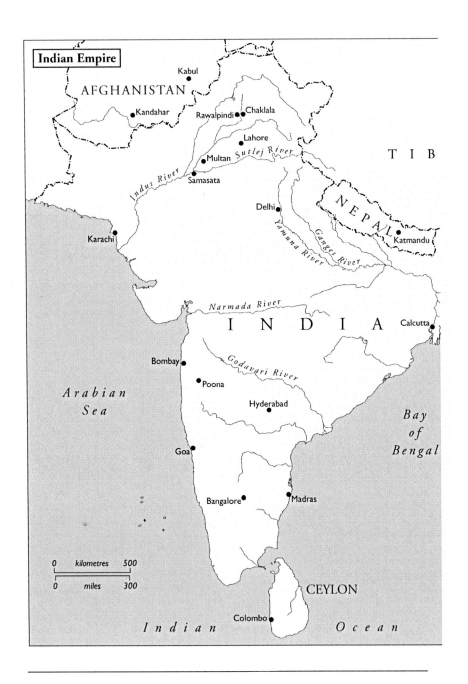

Indian Empire

Kabul

AFGHANISTAN

Kandahar

Rawalpindi • • Chaklala

Lahore

Multan • *Sutlej River*

Indus River

Samasata

Delhi

Yamuna River

Ganges River

T I B

N E P A L

Katmandu

Karachi

Narmada River

I N D I A

Calcutta

Bombay

Godavari River

Poona

*Arabian
Sea*

Hyderabad

*Bay
of
Bengal*

Goa

Bangalore

Madras

| 0 | kilometres | 500 |
| 0 | miles | 300 |

CEYLON

Colombo

Indian   *Ocean*

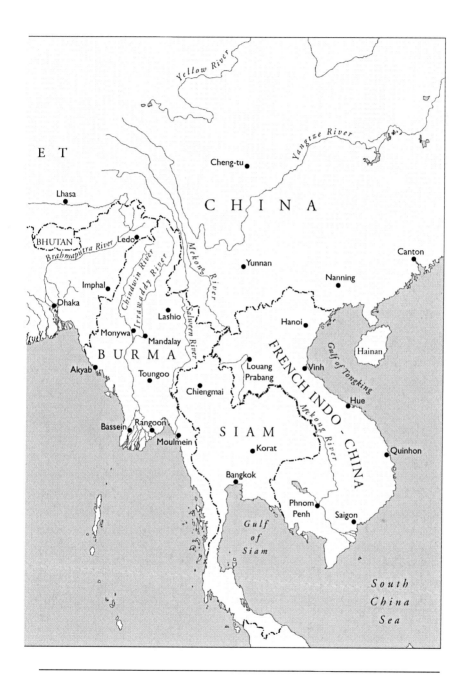

Above: A group photograph of the family taken outside the Post & Telegraph quarters at Rawalpindi some time between 1928 and 1930. From left to right: Eugene, Walter, Cecil Evans, Mother, Richard, Eric and Blanche, with the family dog sitting obediently in front of Walter. Nearly all the photographs in this book were taken on a Brownie Box Camera, which would appear very unsophisticated in comparison with what is available today. Please make due allowance for the period equipment.

1

Early Memories

Rawalpindi, India, 1936

The day we had been awaiting with such anticipation had finally arrived. This evening, my father was taking my sister Blanche and I to visit mother and our new baby sister for the first time and bring them home. With the time now at seven in the morning, however, we had school first. We were eager to leave that morning for we reasoned that the sooner we started the day, the sooner the evening would come when we would see our dear mother again. She seemed to have been away for such a long time although, in fact, she had been in hospital for just over two weeks. We were also longing desperately to see our new baby sister.

We tripped along the path happily – hop, skip, jump, hop, skip, jump – until we reached the crossing before we made our way down the road, racing each other across the big parade ground. It was difficult for Nayeema, our ayah, to keep up with us, hindered as she was by her long-flowing sari and loose sandals – not clothing designed to keep pace with two boisterous young girls, aged nine and six. Mother usually walked us the short distance to and from school, holding our hands and making us walk quietly beside her. Nayeema had now taken on mother's role and we did somewhat take advantage of her by running way ahead.

Today was special. For today was the day father had said he would take us to the hospital to see mother and our new baby sister.

When mother first told us she would be going to hospital and bringing home a new baby, Blanche and I were overjoyed. Babies are so loveable and cuddly – we began making elaborate plans to welcome our new sister. We rummaged through mother's workbox and found an array of fabrics that were left over from the clothes she so skilfully made us. We found skeins of silk thread, fine lace and an assortment of sparkling beads of different colours in that treasure-chest that was her workbasket. Blanche had made a soft rag doll and used brown shaggy wool to form the head. She then dressed it in a little frock, which she trimmed with lace and beads. I wasn't so clever; there was nothing I could make. I could just about thread a darning needle. I searched through my playbox and found a little teddy bear, which I washed carefully before fluffing up the fur with a comb and wrapping it carefully in tissue paper, ready to present to the new baby.

The day passed excruciatingly slowly but at last school was over and, when Nayeema met us, she found she had no need to hurry us along as she usually did on the way home. We ran ahead of her to get back as soon as we could as if that would make the time pass more quickly. A cool drink of limejuice and home-made biscuits awaited us which our cook, Nath, set out for us every day on our return from school.

We waited impatiently for Walter, Eric and Richard to get home. My three elder brothers attended the local senior school and were always late back. Nor had father returned from work; we hoped he would not be delayed today.

The Homecoming, April 1936

When father arrived home from work that memorable day, he had arranged with Abdul to hire a tonga to take us to the hospital. A tonga is a two-wheeled cart. It has some sort of springs by way of suspension, but you would never believe it, even on a smooth road! A tonga is pulled along by a single horse, usually bony and underfed. Not only that, if you happen to be sitting in the front seat next to the tonga-wallah right behind the horse, the smells from its hindquarters are truly disgusting.

The journey to the Holy Family Hospital seemed to take longer than we expected as the horse clip-clopped slowly along the bumpy road, swishing its tail. Before we arrived at the hospital, father told us that mother was very tired, so we were to behave ourselves and be quiet.

We followed the nurse down a long corridor and stopped briefly at the nursery where we looked through the large panes of glass, when she pointed out our baby lying fast asleep in her cot. We then carried on to the ward. Mother looked pale and wan but that did not stop her from greeting us with a hug and a kiss. Then the nurse brought in the baby, all wrapped up in a soft white knitted coverlet and placed her in father's arms.

Mother was thirty-seven years old now and this was the seventh child she had borne. She had not kept very good health for some years. Of late she often said she did not know why she felt so tired, even though she admitted to doing very little. She sometimes needed to go to bed during the day, saying she had had a bad night and felt exhausted.

Today, on leaving the hospital, the doctor said to father, "Your wife, Mr Manuel, has a very delicate constitution. She has had a very difficult delivery. Do not overtax her; she will need plenty of rest and good, nourishing food. I expect her to make a full recovery but if she has any problem do let me know."

A lovely homecoming awaited us when we arrived home. Nath, had prepared a special meal of chicken pillau with brinjal bhurta and all mother's favourite little sweets – hulwa, burfie, gullab jamons. There was so much joy and excitement at mother being home again and, of course, the new baby. We were each allowed to hold our little sister, father warning us that we should not touch the top of her head as it was still soft and tender, adding that in a few weeks' time a protective layer of bone would cover it over completely. We loved her tiny hands that would curl around our fingers. She was gorgeous and would gurgle softly when mother nursed her.

Just a week later, with family and friends, we attended our local church, about a mile and a half away, and celebrated the baptism of Helen Maria.

Indian Summers

The short winters can be quite cold in this part of northern India but in early April the weather changes and the days are pleasantly warm for a few weeks. It had not been long since Blanche and I were in our winter woollies, thick double-breasted overcoats fastened with four large buttons, and the woolly socks and bobble hats that mother made us wear which we stripped off immediately we were out of her sight. Not many of the other children wore hats – we always felt mother made too much fuss. Now though, we could feel spring in our hearts.

Our home was a fairly large single-storey house with four large arches across the front that formed a veranda which shaded the rooms from the bright glare of the sun. Chicks, blinds made of split cane, were fixed across each of the arches. These were rolled and tied up during the cold winter months, but now they had been washed, ready to be let down to keep the rooms cool when the midday sun beat down.

Outside, to the front of the house was a roundel of rose bushes, surrounded by a grassy area that Marlie, the gardener, kept watered and in good condition all the year round. To the right of the path leading to the house were jasmine bushes four feet high, completely covered in tiny white flowers that filled the evening air with a strong perfume. The walls had recently been whitewashed in preparation for the summer and mother's return. Today, the house sparkled in the spring sunshine. Oh, what a perfect homecoming for mother!

My eldest brother Eugene, now sixteen, had already left home and was in the second year of his apprenticeship as a military technician at Chaklala, not many miles from us in Rawalpindi. My father instilled in my brothers the importance of education and training in order for them to be self-reliant by the end of their school life. Eugene was now in this happy situation, self-reliant and enjoying his independence away from home. He was mother's pride and joy: "a good boy – thoughtful, dependable, loyal and hard working." She called him proudly, "The salt of the earth." He was able to come home almost every weekend from his army camp in Chaklala, so the close family bond remained throughout his long absences.

Walter was fifteen and Eric fourteen. Mother always said that they were eternally cooking up some kind of devilment when out of her sight. If there was any rumpus taking place involving children in our local community, she said Walter and Eric would surely be at the heart of it. They would speed alarmingly on their bicycles, zig zagging through tongas, goats, pedestrians and the occasional car, messing about and playing the fool, besides harassing the neighbours with their mischievous ways. However, they were popular with the other children who often joined them in their boisterous fun, frequently ending up in something like a rugby scrum.

Richard, at twelve, was the youngest of my four brothers. He was nearly always in trouble within the family as well as neighbours, and mother said he was disobedient, quick to answer back but slow to learn. He was also very unlucky, for he was nearly always caught red-handed. Forgetful and wilful, he seemed to speed headlong into situations without any thought of the consequences. He was totally without cunning or guile.

While Walter and Eric stuck together and defended each other when they were caught in unruly fun and games, Richard's buddies would completely desert him, leaving him to fend off his adversaries on his own. On numerous occasions, Richard would catch the sting of father's hand across his ear. We loved him dearly and often thought father was not justified in scolding him so severely. To us girls he was the darling of the family, keeping us amused with his daring exploits and tomfoolery. He was always generous with his possessions. We could have the pick of any of his precious playthings, including his vast array of colourful bull's-eye marbles which he had a particular knack of winning.

Generally my three brothers led a carefree and happy life, but some of their games could be quite dangerous. Like many other children of their age, they loved climbing trees and raiding birds' nests and spending long hours playing by the river, trying to catch fish with their bare hands. They made themselves catapults with which to kill birds and often broke windows in the process. Mother had to confiscate these dangerous gadgets when the neighbours complained. She would often have to threaten them by saying she would report them to father.

Blanche, the first girl in the family after four boys, was the favourite, the apple of father's eye, and mother's too.

Father was feared by all the family. He made up for mother's gentleness by meting out severe punishment to the boys by way of a stinging clip across the ear which, coming from him, was quite painful, as Richard would attest.

During the kite season when the wind blew strong at the start of summer, the brothers made their own kites with brilliant-coloured tissue paper, which they pasted over light-weight wooden frames. These they finished off with long bright tails which could be seen for miles around as they spun and fluttered high in the sky, amongst all the other brightly-coloured kites of different shapes and sizes.

One of the games they played was 'Combat Kites', the object of which was to cut the lines of your opponent's kite. In order to prepare the lines for this game, they first dipped the string into home-made glue, which they made by cooking flour and water to a thick gooey consistency. The string was then placed in a bowl of finely crushed glass which was laid it out on the ground in straight lines in the sun to dry. In no time the string was dry and rigid, as sharp as a razor and lethal enough to cut any opponent's kite line. We would all take great delight in watching the kites whose strings they cut being caught in the wind as they floated away far into the distance – lost, perhaps forever.

On one occasion, not knowing what the boys were up to, I wandered into their playroom and, seeing what I thought to be a bowl of sugar, grabbed a handful and stuffed it into my mouth. Of course it was the fine glass powder they used in sharpening their kite lines and all too soon I realised what I had done. I dashed out, spitting out the gritty stuff, thinking I was going to die. I told no one. Hadn't mother warned me often enough to keep away from my brothers and their mischievous schemes, and especially to keep away from their playroom? But I did not take heed of her advice and continued to follow them wherever they went, whenever I could, and became happily involved in all they did.

We enjoyed a comfortable lifestyle, living in the attractive Cantonment area of Rawalpindi where the grounds were tended by marlies whose sole job it was to keep the gardens in good condition all the year round. This housing complex was specially designated for families employed in the Post & Telegraphs Department.

At that time Rawalpindi was a garrison town with a big military presence. The barracks were located just across the road from us where, on special days, interesting activities took place on the parade ground – games, circuses, fêtes, fairs and military men in their colourful uniforms, marching to the accompaniment of stirring bands.

Our small community here consisted mostly of Anglo-Indian families. "Anglo-Indian" is a term difficult to define. We were a minority group of mixed parentage, that is, mostly of English, Portuguese and Indian ancestry, although within my own family I later discovered that my grandparents on my mother's side were, ironically, German and Japanese. Our mother tongue was English, we attended English schools and observed the customs and traditions of what we considered our 'mother country' – Great Britain.

There were a number of Roman Catholic convent schools and colleges scattered throughout the country, as well as schools of other denominations such as the Church of England, the Methodists, The Church of Jesus Christ of Latter-Day Saints and other religious bodies who taught to the same standard and had the same coursework as in Britain. Many of the teachers were from Ireland, France, Belgium and England. Parents had to pay high fees for their children to attend these schools and there were many families who struggled to give their children a good education, as was the case in our household. Sometimes mother would say she found it difficult to 'make ends meet', as there were six of us always in need of clothes and shoes. She would often have a basketful of mending, passing down the clothes worn by my eldest brother to the next in line. She shopped with care, always trying to get the best value for money.

Mother was a tall, slim woman, with dark, kindly eyes and an olive complexion. Her dark hair was neatly cut into the style of the day: a short bob, and whenever she went out she always looked smart and stylish in what she wore. I well remember her dressed in a black and white dress that had a dropped waist and, in front, a black bow. On special occasions, when we went to church, she wore white lacy gloves and a small-rimmed black hat. Unfortunately she suffered with dry skin, sometimes causing her hands and feet to bleed from cracks in her fingers and heels. Part of her daily routine was to rub coconut oil on her hands and feet both morning and night; she had to wear socks and cotton gloves to protect the bedding from oily marks.

Mother was gentle, loving and kindly. Never did we hear a cross word from her, however naughty or high-spirited we were. She never reprimanded us but would reason with us and calmly point out the consequences of our actions.

Mother was obsessively clean and tidy. She would often say, "There's a place for everything and everything should be in its place." She liked to have all her little mementoes and ornaments laid out on the mantelpiece and on her dressing table in a particular way. Even the washing had to be pegged out in a certain way! She was a very caring mother to us all, attending to our every need, but fussed and fretted about everything and everyone. Each morning before breakfast, she would inspect our hands and nails and make sure our shoes were clean. She would brush our hair until it shone, before giving us a big hug, telling us to be good and to listen to our teachers and learn our lessons well, then taking us off to school.

My brothers were often involved in petty squabbles

with the local boys whose verbal abuse in their native tongue would sometimes intimidate them. These brawls caused no end of heartache for mother, for often they would come home with bruises and dirty, torn clothes that she would spend hours trying to patch up.

Mother was an excellent needlewoman and every evening while listening to the radio, she enjoyed working on her embroidery in coloured silks, producing beautiful cushion covers and pillowcases. She had small pieces of fine cotton lawn from which she made delicate handkerchiefs with an embroidered flower in one corner. She also did some fine crochet work which she arranged carefully on various pieces of furniture around the house.

Mother was not a strong woman. She often suffered bouts of illness when she would have to take to her bed. Sometimes father would have to send for the doctor, after which she would be advised to rest and confined to her room for several days. We were never permitted to disturb her during these periods, nor were we told what she was suffering with. Her illness was and still remains a mystery.

Father was a tall man of average build with grey eyes, a brown complexion and dark hair. He wore what mother called a 'Hitler' moustache. He had a direct manner, rigid and inflexible, and would not tolerate anyone defying him or questioning his authority or the decisions he made. He was quite the reverse of mother, with a very strict Victorian attitude towards us children. We would not dream of answering him back on any account; his decision was law and he made no concessions.

On numerous occasions, mother would try to appease father's wrath with some explanation of my brothers' conduct and try to reason with him in her quiet way. But often he would sweep her wishes and arguments aside and punish and – to some degree – bully my brothers into total obedience.

I do not know exactly how my parents met but believe they may have been working together in an office. Mother was twenty when they married, father ten years her senior.

Right: Mother at Rawalpindi in June 1933.

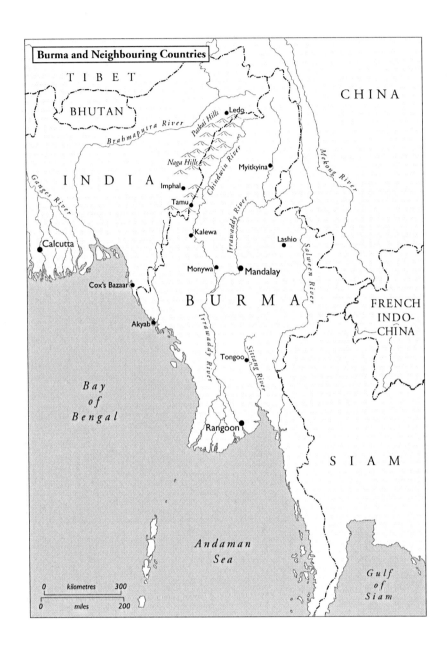

Burma and Neighbouring Countries

TIBET

BHUTAN

CHINA

Brahmaputra River

Patkai Hills

Ledo

Naga Hills

Myitkyina

Chindwin River

INDIA

Imphal

Tamu

Mekong River

Kalewa

Irrawaddy River

Lashio

Ganges River

Calcutta

Monywa

Mandalay

Saluween River

Cox's Bazaar

BURMA

FRENCH
INDO-
CHINA

Akyab

Irrawaddy River

Tongoo

Sittang River

*Bay
of
Bengal*

Rangoon

SIAM

*Andaman
Sea*

*Gulf
of
Siam*

| 0 | kilometres | 300 |
| 0 | miles | 200 |

Left: Blanche holding Helen at the headquarters building of the Post & Telegraphs Department, Monywa, 1939

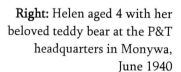

Right: Helen aged 4 with her beloved teddy bear at the P&T headquarters in Monywa, June 1940

Above: A Burmese paddy boat on the River Chindwin at Monywa; the date is unknown but must be between the family's arrival in 1937 and departure in 1942. The Chindwin formed the first part of the children's escape route from Burma.

2

Transfer to Burma

It was about a year after Helen was born that father was offered a position by way of promotion, to Burma. An opportunity such as this that would advance his career prospects in the Post & Telegraphs Department did not often arise. Here in Rawalpindi, there was not much chance of achieving promotion; progress in the department looked bleak. He knew of a number of his colleagues who had transferred to Burma, who not only improved their promotional prospects, but also told of the pleasant and enjoyable lifestyle they led there. So, after considerable discussions with mother as to what might be best for the needs of the growing family and having her full support, he applied for the vacant post in Mandalay.

After a few months of waiting, father received news that he had been accepted for the post and soon preparations were being made for the move. The thought of living in a new country so far away seemed a wonderfully exciting prospect for us all.

We were full of questions: we asked: "Where exactly

is Burma, Daddy?" "How far is it from here?" "How will we get there?" "Will we have a new house?" "Do they speak a different language?" "Will we have to speak Burmese?"

Father brought out a large map of the Indian subcontinent. He explained that all the area coloured pink on the map that included India and Burma formed part of the British Empire and traced out the route our journey was likely to take to our destination in Mandalay.

"From here in Rawalpindi in the far north-west of India, we will travel south-east by train through Delhi, then follow the valley of the River Ganges, through Benares and continue eastwards towards Calcutta. We will board a small ship in Calcutta and travel south, round the Bay of Bengal, to Rangoon, the capital of Burma." He added, "If time allows, we might take a short break before taking the train on to Mandalay." It looked a very long journey.

En Route to Calcutta, May, 1937

When the manager of the removal firm came to assess our belongings, he assured mother that his company had been transporting the household effects of kings and queens, and a whole host of regiments besides, since the year 1758. He proudly added: "You can rest assured, Mrs Manuel, that not so much as a single cup has been broken in all that time!" Mother felt happy to entrust our furniture and household effects to the care of Cox & Kings, removal specialists.

So began our journey to father's new posting in

Mandalay. There were six of us children – Walter, Eric, Richard, Blanche, Helen and myself, our ages ranging from fifteen years to one. Our cook, Juggernath, or Nath as we affectionately called him, also accompanied us. He had become an integral part of the family over the years, having been with us for as long as I could remember – a big man, dark and strong with black wispy hair and a strong bass voice.

Eugene was also on the train as we left Rawalpindi; he had spent a short period of leave with us and was now returning to his regiment, the Royal Electrical & Mechanical Engineers (REME), stationed at Chaklala.

When the train stopped at Chaklala there was a quiet, sombre parting. He would not be able to visit us in Mandalay as he was still in training and the journey would be too far for him to make within the short periods of his leave. I can still remember how smart he looked, tall and handsome in his starched uniform, his highly polished boots and the brass buttons on his jacket and cap badge sparkling in the sunshine. Mother could not hide her tears as the train slowly pulled away from the platform, leaving Eugene looking sad and alone as we waved him goodbye.

All the windows of the carriage were opened to disperse the hot air as the train chugged slowly along through the scrub of the flat plain. Despite the heat, we were excited and exhilarated at the thrill of the journey and the constantly changing scene outside from vast flat scrubland to the fertile valley of the Ganges.

We were indeed fortunate that father was entitled to

first-class travel; to have the privilege of a compartment to ourselves, to stretch and move about in comfort and have Nath bring us meals and snacks from tea-rooms located on platforms. Also throughout the journey, father ordered huge block of ice, on sale at most railway stations during the summer months, which were placed in metal trays to bring the temperature down by a few degrees. What is more, we could put our hot sticky fingers on the ice blocks to cool our hands and faces.

We could not help noticing that some compartments on the train were crowded with people packed tightly together carrying chickens, goats and other livestock as well as bedding rolls and bundles of possessions, passively enduring the sweltering heat of the day.

The stale sweaty smell of humanity and livestock filled the air as we stepped off the train on to the crowded platform at Calcutta, just occasionally relishing the whiff of perfume from garlands of flowers that some passengers were being welcomed with by relatives or friends. After four days on the train we were hot and tired and much in need of quiet rest and cool refreshment.

Calcutta was, and still is, a large busy city teeming with people. So much hustle and bustle, tongas, oxcarts, rickshaws pulled along by thin muscular men and cyclists weaving in and out of heavy traffic, as well as sacred Brahmin bulls and cows that appeared to take precedence over all.

Mother was most distressed at the sight of so many beggars on street corners, so many poor and hungry people, so many hapless children without limbs. "Whatever will become of these innocent souls?" she wondered. But father tried to distract us from the street scene by pointing out the many large imposing buildings on either side of the main street. "Look at all these lovely buildings, so solidly built in red brick, so sound and stable," he said. "They're most likely to be here for many a long year."

En Route to Rangoon, May 1937

After a short break, we continued on our journey, embarking on what seemed to be a very large ship. I cannot remember the name, but father said it was a modern vessel providing every amenity we could wish for. The passengers on board were mostly prosperous-looking Europeans and Indians. There were also families like us who were taking up posts in Burma. We were to spend four days on this luxurious cruise ship.

I remember most of this wondrous journey. Our family was allotted two comfortable sleeping cabins side by side, and we were thrilled at their spaciousness. The playroom was stacked with more games and toys than we could ever have imagined. The boys took full advantage of the competitive games involving tests of skill – quoits, billiards and darts – during which time they made many friends on board. We never tired of exploring the ship from top to bottom with its many nooks and crannies; more to discover than we had ever thought possible. Eric, Walter and

Richard explored every section, once creeping down an iron staircase towards the engine room, attracted by the noise and the smell of grease and oil. They were quickly caught and chased out by a member of the crew before they could get close enough to see the working heart of the ship.

Rangoon, May 1937

We were now approaching the port of Rangoon, which is located in the flat low-lying area forming the delta region of Burma. There were many large ships and hundreds of little boats plying up and down the river, some housing families, their colourful washing fluttering on clothes-lines on tiny decks. It took us some hours to arrive at the main seaport where the larger ships and barges were moored.

We were sad to disembark from this great ship. It had been such a wonderful experience; the days had gone by all too quickly. Now we were packing up our bits and pieces, vacating our cabins and getting ready for the next leg of our journey, with mother carrying Helen and fretting in case we had left any of our belongings behind in the cabins.

As we travelled along to our hotel, the streets were full of people bustling about in pursuit of their daily business. We were fascinated to see how the Burmese were dressed, the men in their lungies, very loose skirts which were tied in a knot at the front. They wore funny little white cotton triangular hats, knotted at each corner to fit the head, or so it seemed. The women wore lungies with neat, colourful tops, and nearly all were carrying brightly coloured waxed parasols to protect themselves from the blazing sun.

We wondered why they wore rather streaky, creamy makeup smeared over their faces and were later told that it was called Tha-na-kah, made from the bark of a tree similar to sandalwood, which is ground on a stone with a little water, to a fine paste. It is said to have a cooling effect on the skin.

We passed a number of beautiful golden pagodas, shimmering in the early evening sun. At the entrance to each pagoda crouched a pair of horrendous-looking statues called Chintheys, mythological beasts, half-lion and half-griffin, which stand guard to ward off evil spirits.

Our hotel formed part of a Victorian building and, when we entered the large lobby, we marvelled at the intricate wrought-iron staircase that wound its way grandly to the first floor. We were led to the two rooms allocated to us by a young man wearing a black and white uniform and a smart red turban. The rooms were large and airy with French windows opening on to a small balcony overlooking a busy street.

The following day, father took us on a tour of the city. He pointed out the many fine architectural features of the Victorian buildings lining the main thoroughfare. He said that after the British conquered the town in 1824, they designed and supervised the building of roads in a grid fashion. We were struck in awe and wonder at the beauty of the many golden pagodas we saw dazzling in the sunshine, especially the most stunning of all, the Shwedagon Pagoda, with its tall golden pinnacle and immense Chintheys at the entrance. Inside, people were laying garlands of flowers, lighting joss sticks and candles, and praying before a massive Buddha. Hazy smoke from the many joss sticks gave out a strong, heady odour whilst making patterns against the dark interior and creating an atmosphere of calm and tranquillity.

We spent two idyllic days in Rangoon but had to leave this lovely city too soon, as the time for father to take up his new post was drawing near and we still had a distance of about 400 miles to travel by train.

Mandalay, June, 1937

The mountain ranges of Burma run from north to south and break up the country into valleys traversed by three rivers. The Irrawaddy – Burma's greatest river – has its source in the mountainous region of China in the southern Himalayas and cuts a swathe through the middle of the country for about 1,350 miles, dividing and spreading itself into a delta 150 miles wide in the south before it reaches the Andaman Sea. Called 'The Road to Mandalay' by British colonialists, this river has been the land's major transportation route. The River Chindwin also has its source in China and flows down from the northern tip of Burma through the Hnkawng Valley and close to the pass known as Ledo Road. It winds its way westward through ranges of mountains near the border with India and then into the plains, joining the Irrawaddy southwest of Mandalay. The third river, the Salween, also originates in China in the north-east, very close to what is known as the Burma Road, and flows through the lush and beautiful Shan States where the finest rubies are mined.

As we sped past through the countryside, it looked lush and verdant with vast wetlands of paddy fields, rice being the main crop of the region. The weather was comfortably warm, different to the dry heat of India. Father told us that in the summer months when the monsoon strikes, the rain falls in torrential downpours. He said it caused the rivers to flow with great force and nearly every year the low-lying areas were flooded for miles around. It is for this reason that many of the wooden houses along the riverbank are built on stilts about six feet off the ground.

Mandalay, known as the 'Golden City' for its many golden pagodas and temples, is a thriving place, bustling with life. The main street is wide and lined with palm trees. There are large imposing colonial buildings of red brick on both sides of the road. Father said there were many British and European families living and working here. He pointed out a few big houses at the end of long drives, some built in the Tudor style. We glimpsed a derelict fortress some distance away surrounded by smaller dilapidated outbuildings where in ancient times, father said, the King of Burma lived with his large entourage. We also passed many solid-looking ancient Buddhist monuments.

There were people of other cultures living and working here in harmony alongside the native Burmese – many Indians and people from Indo-China. The Chinese had a big presence in the town with their large shops selling rich silks, intricately carved ivory and beautifully carved furniture.

We passed many churches with high, ornate steeples. Father said many of them were designed and built by Italians, with marble altars, pillars and porticoes.

We were excited at seeing the natural lush green of our new environment as father explained the interesting details of the landscape and buildings throughout the journey.

Above: The imposing exterior of Mandalay railway station in 1937. Note the horse-drawn carriages on the right.

3

Monywa, Burma

We were destined not to stay many months in Mandalay, for my father was instructed to take up a new post in Monywa by way of further promotion. Mother had barely settled into our new home when she had to pack up our belongings and think of our next move. Her main concern was that our education would again be disrupted. A suitable school where lessons were taught in English would have to be found. Father assured her that she would get help with the packing; she was not to worry. He would also make sure that we were all placed in schools where we would get a good English education.

Monywa is 85 miles north-west of Mandalay on the eastern bank of the River Chindwin, a tributary of the Irrawaddy. It is a typical small town with rows of detached houses, nearly all built of teak and having gardens large enough to grow exotic fruit trees – mango, jack fruit, tall coconut trees, toddy palms, and banana trees.

Our new home was a substantial two-storey, teakwood building, the first floor having a covered veranda all round. "This house had been designed and built by a Chinese architect," said our landlord Mr Wong, proudly. The first floor was the main living area, the rooms being large with dark polished teak floors. In one corner of the front veranda was a small platform jutting out, about two feet square, built in the style of a miniature pagoda and forming a shrine – a spirit house. It had a square roof of nine levels, tapering into a spike and painted bright red and gold. It was the custom to place a statue of Buddha in the spirit house. A chirag – a tiny earthenware saucer filled with oil – would be lit every night to ward off evil spirits. On special feast days, there would be offerings of flowers and incense, which gave off a strong heady smell. This type of structure was built into every dwelling in this district where the inhabitants were nearly all Buddhists.

The lounge was large and comfortable, and father was very proud of his new short-wave radio – an Eddystone All-World Eight that he installed soon after we moved in. He rigged up a most complicated aerial that was strung between posts twenty feet high, suspended above the garden and extending 60 feet across. It was powered by a one-hundred-torch battery unit housed in a wooden box, and every evening we were made to sit quietly and listen to classical music from the Overseas Service of the BBC. We were also made to sit, too often, to listen to "World Affairs" by Wickham Steed, and other news broadcasts from London which we could barely understand.

In the lounge hung a large oval oil painting of mother and father when they were first married. My father had commissioned an American artist to paint the picture, which the artist had enlarged from a small photograph. It was a beautiful painting and one of our most treasured possessions. On either side of the door leading into mother's dressing room were a pair of Japanese vases that stood about two feet high. They were of the finest porcelain, intricately painted in bright colours. Blanche and I loved to follow the raised edges of the flowers and birds with our fingers on these lovely pieces, and tried to trace them into our books. There were also many fine Chinese pictures of flowers, delicately embroidered on fine silk, which hung on various walls.

We were convinced that the anteroom off mother's dressing room was haunted, and many times in the middle of the night I woke Blanche to ask if she could hear the sound of a walking stick, tap-tapping up and down the little room. Mother said it was all in our imagination, but we were very frightened of what we were sure was a ghost making its presence known after dark, but too scared to get out of bed to investigate.

Scare stories to do with ghosts and evil spirits proliferated in our local community. During our walks in the street we would often pass an attractively arranged bunch of flowers, or a tempting bowl of sweets left by the side of a road. Nath, in one of his more serious tones, told us never to touch anything left in the street. He said, "This is the work of the devil. There are evil people who practise black magic of the most dangerous kind. These tempting bits are left by sick people who want you to pick them up and take them home." he said. "If you were to take the flowers or eat the sweets you will get their illness for sure and the evil person who placed them there will recover. This is the way it works. You better believe it! You must never touch anything left by the roadside." He emphasised his words by shaking his finger and opening his eyes so wide that we could see the whites of them. We did not doubt him for a moment; we took him very seriously, for the casting of spells and stories of black magic were rife among our friends. If you were to ask me if I believe in ghosts, black magic or whether it was possible to cast evil spells on your enemies or those you envied, I would say, "Yes, I certainly do."

The first time Mr. Wong showed us round the ground floor he advised father not to place anything of value in these rooms. He said that two years ago, after a period of heavy rain, the rooms were flooded to a depth of several feet. A great deal of damage had been done to some heavy furniture that could not be moved before the water overwhelmed the area. "Treat these rooms as empty spaces," he advised. "Once the monsoon rain starts it comes down in torrents and if it gets flooded you may not have time to move anything." He said two people who had been working in the fields near the river were swept away and sadly lost their lives.

So the ground floor was left bare with the exception of bits of old furniture. However, there was a small, damp, windowless room in the far corner that housed some large earthenware jars, about four feet tall and two feet in diameter that belonged to the landlord. He said that he would have them removed within weeks, so father made no objection to them being left and assured the landlord that the children would not be allowed entry into this room.

However, not many months went by before we were wondering what might be in these jars in this forbidden room. So one day when father was out, and having the curious and disobedient brothers that I did, Richard, Walter and Eric decided to pick the lock. We crept into the dark room and discovered there were six jars containing a thick brownish substance called jaggery (palm sugar). It had a strong sickly sweet smell. Eric tasted it and said it was horrible – sickeningly sweet and rancid. Suddenly Nath appeared and caught us red-handed. I don't think he was surprised to see us there, with Eric in the act of tasting the contents, but he did give us a good telling off. Nath himself was quite intrigued by the secret of the locked room, so he also took a look and said he could not be sure but thought there was something nasty and illegal happening here. It looked like some kind of illicit alcoholic brew in the making. "Why did Mr Wong not store the jars in his own large house or in one of the outbuildings?" Nath wondered. "He did not want to be caught out, that's why!" he said, answering his own question.

Nath, the font of all knowledge and understanding, did not report the incident to father but locked the door securely and, rolling his dark eyes wide, warned us never to go in there again. "Besides," he said, shaking his finger at us, "it's full of creepy-crawlies, with scorpions and snakes lurking in corners behind the smelly jars - so stay out!"

The kitchen was in a separate building, to the rear of the house. It had a cooking range of four coal-burning fires. Nath, who had originally come from Madras and had accompanied our family from Rawalpindi, was a large jolly man with a deep bass voice that trembled as he sang his Tamil songs. We treated him as a friend, a confidant and an integral part of the family, taking father's place in protecting us in his absence when duty took him up country away from home. Besides being an excellent cook, he was honest, hardworking and loyal, and very much concerned for the welfare of the family in times of trouble. Even when father was at home and the boys were about to be punished for some small misdemeanour, it was usually Nath who tried to cover up for them and defend them from our strict father.

On one occasion after a downpour of rain, during a squabble between Richard and Eric when they were throwing sticks and stones at each other, Richard threw Eric's shoes high on to the kitchen roof. When Eric climbed up to retrieve them, he slipped off the wet tiles and came crashing down, fracturing his arm and twisting his ankle. Nath was the first on the scene, the curry he was preparing on the fire left to burn in his haste to accompany mother and Eric to hospital. When they returned, Nath was more concerned that the punishment Richard would surely get was likely to be more painful than Eric's injuries. He was right, for when father returned from work and saw Eric's arm and leg bandaged and heard that Richard was the cause of it all, Richard was severely punished, despite mother's pleas in trying to defend him, saying it was the normal behaviour of boisterous boys.

To the front of the kitchen was a covered veranda that made a good shelter from the hot sun. From time to time, travelling craftsmen would call to carry out various household repairs. A man wearing a turban and thin cotton shirt and loose white pants would come to mend father's watch or mother's sewing machine. The cobbler was a regular caller with his last and assorted tools to mend our shoes. The carpenter would set up his lathe and turn out a perfectly matching leg to replace a broken one for a chair or table. The bedding man would set up his big wooden frame which had a tight wire strung across it that he twanged like a guitar, fluffing up the cotton filling from mattresses or teasing the feathers from pillows. It was wonderful, feathers flying everywhere. He would then pack the cleaned filling into new ticking, carefully measuring and stitching it to the right size so that at the end of the process it was as good as new. We watched in fascination as these roving tradesmen carried out their work with such remarkable skill.

Throughout the months we spent in this house we made full use of the vacant rooms on the ground floor. Most of the space became a play area except for one room which Walter, Eric and Richard converted into a workshop. Their hobby was woodwork. They fixed up shelves and benches, set up their tools and fretwork saws, and tins of paint of various colours were all arranged in neat rows. They spent many happy hours making toys, which made very acceptable presents for friends and neighbours. They made a set of Snow White and the Seven Dwarfs cut from plywood, painting each piece in colours that were matched exactly to the original Disney characters. I well remember them being fixed in a row against the wall above my bed. We were of course familiar with the children's stories of the day and enjoyed reading and being read to by mother. My brothers also made a little cot for Blanche's doll, which mother finished off by sewing a cotton lining and trimming it with lace. Mother encouraged the boys in their hobby and said how proud she was of their creative skills.

We often had our Burmese and Chinese neighbours join us in boisterous and noisy games, chasing each other in and out of the rooms on the ground floor when the sun beat down mercilessly outside. There were so many rooms, so many doors, so many corners and pieces of unwanted furniture to jump over and hide behind.

On one such occasion when we were playing hide-and-seek, I was about to hide behind a door when suddenly I found myself staring at a snake – curled upwards, face to face almost – its flat head swaying slightly to and fro. I stopped, petrified, completely mesmerised by it. I could not utter a sound. I don't know how long I may have stood there in a trance; maybe just a few seconds, but it seemed an eternity before the others realised there was something wrong. It was Eric who happened to be nearby and, spotting the menacing, hissing snake as it swayed preparing to strike, quickly pushed me away and yelled to the others. Suddenly there was the clatter of broomsticks; garden forks and spades as they chased the speeding, writhing creature from room to room. It was some time before it succumbed to the battering from all sides and, when eventually my brothers and their friends laid out the snake to its full length on the ground outside for all to see, it measured over six feet. All our friends, neighbours, servants, and mother and father gathered round to examine the creature and thank God that no one had been hurt in the mayhem. The snake was later discovered to be a cobra with its spectacled, hooded flat head. Had it put its fangs into any of us the outcome might well have turned out to be fatal, for we were many miles from any hospital.

The garden consisted of small strips of land on either side with a larger area at the back, all enclosed within a low picket fence. The small banana tree did not as yet bear fruit but the large leaves gave some shade from the sun. The custard-apple tree in one corner by the gate bore the most luscious creamy-sweet fruit. To the rear of the house, the large tamarind tree spread its leaves like giant lace ferns, high and wide.

During the school holidays we waited for various vendors to call with their tasty snacks, with little cakes and sweetmeats arranged in flat baskets which they carried on their heads. We begged mother for a few pice to buy a treat, but most times she said no, it was not safe to eat, we could catch some terrible disease. She was conscious of the dangers of buying from street vendors and the health hazards they posed. Just a few weeks before, a little girl in our neighbourhood had died of Black Water Fever. We also heard of the deaths from other diseases in this locality. Rats and mice were particularly dreaded, as it was well known that they were the cause of smallpox, cholera and other serious diseases. But in spite of her advice, to have a surreptitious taste of the most delicious ice cream, drizzled with sweet vanilla sauce when the weather was steaming hot, was a treat beyond compare.

Many of the houses in this part of the town had no electricity or running water and sanitation was primitive, the 'night soil' being taken away in the dead of night.

When we looked down from our balcony on the first floor, we could watch the antics of children and adults around a standpipe located in front of our house where local people collected their fresh water in buckets, jugs and earthenware pots, called chatties. Many used their buckets to pour water over themselves straight from the tap, the men with lungies tied round their middle, and the women wearing their colourful lungies knotted over their bosom.

In April, at full moon, the Burmese celebrate the Buddhist New Year with a water-throwing festival lasting three days. The old year must be washed away with water; the New Year anointed with water. The trick is to catch people out by throwing buckets of water, often coloured with red or yellow dye, when they least expect it. You can be walking down the street in your best suit and when you turn a corner you are suddenly confronted with someone throwing brightly coloured water at you. No one is safe from the soaking that can come from any direction. At times it can be very annoying. From the young girl carrying a pot on her head to the skinny street cleaner labouring with his bucket, everyone is a potential prankster who might at any moment drench you from head to toe. It was all great fun for the children but well known for businesses, farm labour and even governments to come to a virtual standstill during this festival.

The Festival of Light was celebrated at the end of the Buddhist lent with the sighting of the full moon in September or October. Millions of candles and little oil lamps are lit outside monasteries, pagodas and even placed in trees, and every house is decorated with tiny clay pots placed along the railings of verandas. It makes a spectacular scene of twinkling lights, near and far. Inevitably, some of the timber-built houses caught fire and burned fiercely, often spreading to neighbouring houses and causing considerable damage.

Our Chinese landlord, Mr Wong, lived in a large house next door. He was a small bald man with a kindly round face and a huge belly. He had a tall, attractive, much younger wife. Her long jet-black hair was always neatly plaited and arranged in a bun. She visited mother occasionally and brought her flowers when she was ill. They had four children who often joined us in our boisterous games.

Opposite our house was a large grassed area in the middle of which was a huge banyan tree where children from the neighbourhood played ball games: rounders and gully-dunda, a similar game to cricket. During the hottest part of the day, the men would gather round to sit in the shade of the tree, whiling away the afternoon.

Just beyond the grassy area to the front of our house

was a Buddhist temple where the monks, dressed in saffron-coloured robes, their heads shaven, walked up and down their garden in the cool of the evening, prayer beads in their hands, chanting their mantra.

Generally speaking, we did not mix with the local people except for casual greetings when passing them in the street. We learned little of their language, their culture being so very different from ours. In this particular area of Monywa, the local people looked upon us as strangers and foreigners, for we dressed in western clothes, spoke English and came from India.

Mother had just a handful of loyal friends and she would often take us – Blanche, Helen and me – with her when she went visiting. Friends would occasionally take us out to the countryside in their cars for picnics, but not as often as we would have wished. At home, mother was always busy. Every morning she would take out her notebook and sit with Nath to plan the shopping needs of the day. When Nath returned from the bazaar with the groceries, he would have to account for every pice. There were times when it seemed a struggle for mother to work out how best to feed the family. At the end of the week, there were often times when she said she did not have enough to pay the dhobi (washer man) and she and Miriam, the ayah, would have to do a huge wash, rubbing and scrubbing every piece of clothing by hand. In the steaming heat of summer, this was no easy job and, by the end, she would be quite exhausted and spend the rest of the evening in bed. But despite our money problems, there was always food on the table, and sometimes a few treats. We did not own a car but tongas were convenient and cheap to hire.

Late June saw the onset of the monsoon season. Though this is an annual occurrence, it always seemed to catch us unawares. On that first day, the heavens opened and the rain poured down like bullets from a darkened sky.

The few people filling their buckets and pots from the tap outside ran for shelter under the banyan tree, but slowly dispersed when there was no let-up in the downpour. Soon water was running off the roofs and collecting in pools round the houses. Before long, it had started running down the street in little rivulets.

Father grew worried as the rain continued to pour down for the next few hours. We were quite close to the river and he wondered if we should move further away. He discussed the situation with mother who was reluctant to move at first, but he said if the rain didn't stop and the water level rose any higher the river could burst its banks, as had happened a couple of years ago, and we could be marooned here for days. We might not then be able to leave except in small boats. Besides, the drinking water could become contaminated and our health put at risk. Mother could not disagree with him. She fully realised it would be hazardous to our health if we stayed here any longer, for we were very aware of the danger from waterborne diseases. Father said the time had come to think seriously about making some contingency plans.

Discussions with our landlord soon followed and he approved father's plan to find a place further away from the river. He said this monsoon rain was similar to what had been experienced exactly two years ago. He said he would assess the situation in the morning and might consider moving his own family elsewhere if the rain had not eased off by then.

When we awoke the following morning the street was awash with water to a depth of about four inches. There were desperate-looking people in the street outside, struggling to fill jugs and bottles with water from the tap. Some women were splashing through the water carrying babies on their hips and bundles on their heads, obviously having to leave their homes to find higher ground.

Father left early that day to put his plan into action, for there was no let-up in the constant downpour. He told mother to have us all ready to leave later that morning. He said he would organise somewhere for us to stay. He would try to get us temporarily housed in one of the dāk bungalows. These were small fully-equipped bungalows especially set aside for overnight accommodation for visiting dignitaries of the Post & Telegraphs Department, or emergencies such as this.

It was later in the morning, as the floodwater was rising in the street and had started lapping the front of the building, that father arrived with two tongas. We quickly piled inside, mother making sure we were each carrying our own little bag of belongings, Helen clutching tightly on to her big teddy bear. Our ayah, Miriam, and Nath were also with us, carrying tinned foodstuffs, a selection of spices, a few pots and pans and some of their personal belongings.

The monsoon lasted for about five weeks during which time we stayed in the dāk bungalow in rather cramped conditions. At the end of this period, the landlord got in touch with father to tell him the floodwater had receded and the house was dry and habitable. It had been cleaned and whitewashed, ready for us to move back, he said. But when we went to inspect it prior to moving in, mother and father were both horrified. It had obviously not been properly cleaned and the ground floor felt sticky underfoot. Myriads of flies had collected round the door of the little room and a horrible sickly smell pervaded the whole place. It transpired that the rainwater had inundated the ground floor, including the little room, and swamped the jars. The liquefied jaggery had overflowed, forming a thick liquid that had spread throughout the ground floor. In some corners it had started to dry up. The whole place was swarming with flies.

"Look at this, Mr. Wong," mother said, pointing to the sticky floor, the flies and the dirty tide mark seven feet high along the wall. "You cannot possibly expect us to move into this place. The children use this as a play area; they spend a lot of time down here. It is most unhygienic. Please have it cleaned up properly." Father too was furious at seeing the condition of the house and insisted that it be cleaned up thoroughly before we returned. The landlord was most apologetic and promised that he would make sure the place was cleaned to our satisfaction. Father later said the landlord could not have inspected the house in the first place. How he could expect anyone to live in a house in such a state was inconceivable. "It's revolting, disgusting," he added.

When father had made a thorough inspection a few weeks later, he was able to assure mother that the floor had been cleaned and the walls properly washed and disinfected. Unfortunately, the delicate silk embroidered pictures downstairs were ruined. But father was satisfied that it was now in a good clean condition, ready for us to move in, except for the jars which he said Mr Wong would remove within the next few weeks. However, many months were to elapse before the unpleasant smell disappeared and my brothers continued to frighten us, saying that there were snakes and scorpions lurking in all the corners of the dark windowless room at the back.

Monywa, October, 1938

At about this time there was much comment in the local newspapers and on radio calling for independence for Burma. Mother and father felt it was increasingly likely to affect us as 'foreigners'. We heard of numerous instances of stone-throwing and verbal abuse towards the Anglo-Indian and Indian communities, and possibly towards other migrant workers as well. Petty brawls with the local people were becoming ever more frequent on the street and Nath said there were constant squabbles and disputes in the bazaars between Indian shopkeepers and the Burmese.

Our family too was caught up in these feelings of hostility, living as we did in an area where the population was predominantly Burmese. When Walter, Richard and Eric walked home from school, they were often the butt of verbal abuse from street children, and sometimes pelted with stones, in much the same way as we were when we walked to school with mother or Miriam. We would turn a corner only to be confronted by a group of young boys taunting us by shouting abuse or hurling stones at us. At that time, we could not understand the reason we were being singled out and were often close to tears on reaching school.

The saffron-robed monks from the Buddhist temple opposite our home were also showing their resentment at us being there by stamping their feet when passing us in the street, shouting and shaking their clenched fists. Sometimes they would even throw stones at our house for reasons we could not fathom.

On one occasion, when relations between the Burmese and Indians were particularly tense and there had been several reports of rioting in the village, Nath, having just returned from the bazaar, excitedly told father that he had heard some disturbing news circulating that morning concerning the monks from the monastery opposite.

"My friend Saleem overheard some men talking together in the bazaar, sahib," he said anxiously. "The monks are planning to break into this house and attack us at night with dahs and force us to leave. They might even try to kill us. They call us foreign pigs and infidels. These are not rumours, sahib, this is very serious. You must take it seriously. The situation in the street is worse than we thought. I hear it all the time. We are particularly targeted because of our proximity to the temple. They resent us living here. They want to be rid of us. We must leave and go to a safer place soon, sahib, soon!"

It was by good fortune that father was home that particular day and not away on tour for weeks. Nor did he take Nath's story lightly. The killing of entire families on the whim of a few enraged individuals was not unknown. Here, life was cheap when passions were inflamed. The monks, in spite of their high ideals and contemplative lives of peace, serenity and silence, were human after all and, in the cause of self-government, possessed the same hostile antagonism towards foreign nationals as those around them, perhaps even more so than the man in the street. This feeling was not new; it had been rumbling on for many years. 'Go Home', 'Quit Burma', 'Self-Rule for Burma' read many a banner and newspaper headline.

The following day, father went to see our landlord. Mr Wong said he had also encountered threatening behaviour towards his family from the local people. Like us, he was considered a 'foreigner'. He too had been planning to move his family away from the area. Wealthy Chinese traders, like the Indian shopkeepers, were being threatened openly. "Go home," they said. "You are taking away business from the local Burmese people."

Father wasted no time in making enquiries about alternative accommodation for the family, preferably near his place of work. The apartment above his office seemed the obvious choice, being a short distance away from the police station and the barracks of the Indian Sikh Infantry

Regiment. As the apartment had been vacant for some time, he was able to arrange for us to move in immediately.

We did, in fact, move hurriedly, taking with us just a few necessities. Not long after this, father arranged for our belongings to be moved to our new abode. Mother found the apartment a bit cramped, having six children at home still, but she was much happier in this safer environment. We were now out of sight of the Buddhist monastery and there was a marked improvement in her health. We later heard that the monks, accompanied by other men of the district, had indeed raided our house in the dead of night wielding dahs, truncheons and knives. There can be little doubt that they would have crept up the stairs and attempted to kill us all in our beds in what was fast becoming a dangerous and lawless society.

Walter and Eric Leave Home, January, 1941

Walter was now aged nineteen and father was keen for him to start thinking of his future and earning his own living. He advised Walter to try for an apprenticeship within the Post & Telegraphs Department and, after a number of enquiries and some research, Walter applied for a vacancy in Maymyo, north-east of Mandalay. Water was interested in studying Radio Transmission and Physics and was told that, if he could obtain the necessary textbooks for the course, a place could be found for him. These particular textbooks could not be bought in Burma, so Walter contacted Eugene in India and asked him if he could send out the books, which fortunately Eugene was able to do just before the start of the course.

Walter worked hard, putting in hours of extra study and gaining a good result in his examination, after which he was posted to Lashio, a small town in the north-east at the foothills of the Himalayan mountain range and some distance from Maymyo.

Eric, aged eighteen, was also sent to undergo his apprenticeship in the Post & Telegraphs Department, but he chose to go to Rangoon. In the course of his study, in spite of the meagre wages he received and the hardship of his living conditions, his perseverance and hard work was rewarded for he obtained a high grade in his final examination.

The departure of both Walter and Eric at about the same time was a great loss to us at home. Mother in particular worried about their welfare, living and working as they were in unfamiliar places, so far away from home. Were they eating properly? Taking proper care of themselves? She spoke often of her fears. The house seemed empty and deserted without them. Blanche, Helen and I missed all the games we played and their brotherly protection as they accompanied us on walks, especially now that every news broadcast told of worrying stories of senseless attacks against foreigners and warning that extra care should be taken when travelling to certain areas of the country.

The family led a fairly normal and uneventful life for a few years. We had the use of the large garden where we raised chickens in the hen house and ducks in the pond. A turkey would be bought a few weeks before Christmas and fattened up in preparation for the big day.

Father would often let Nath off his kitchen duties and take over the kitchen. He was an exceptionally good cook and made delicious pickles and chutneys. In October he would shop in the local bazaar to chose the best ingredients for the annual Christmas cake. A batch of seven cakes would be baked at the same time, one for each of our birthdays. We delighted in helping him chop up almonds, angelica and all the other ingredients that went into making them. He answered all our questions and explained in detail the reason why the flour had to be sifted three times and why raisins and sultanas had to be de-seeded, washed and dried carefully. These were joyful occasions for us all.

I remember that father was a kind and loving man towards mother. He adored her and carried out her every wish during his 'normal' days, but often lacked patience and tolerance towards us children. I grew up to be quite frightened of him. To me he was not a loving father but a big scary presence. I cannot recall being held by him or sitting on his knee or even being noticed by him. He did not show any affection towards us children, with the exception of Blanche, for she was his favourite, perhaps being the first born girl after four sons.

It was mother who took total charge of nurturing us, demonstrating much love and affection in everything she did. She listened, supported and disciplined us in a quiet, unruffled way, explaining with great sensitivity the rights and wrongs of our occasional unruly behaviour.

My father's job in the Post & Telegraphs Department in Monywa was the supervision, inspection, maintenance and installation of telephone and telegraph lines in addition to being head of the telegraph office. The district of his administration covered the rugged, mountainous region north of Monywa. He had a team of coolies and linesmen who accompanied him on these tours, which took him away from home for periods of two or three weeks at a time.

It may have been from pressure of work, frustration, his many responsibilities or conditions up country, but my father was invariably in a shocking mood on his return home. He seemed to change from a caring father to a frightening, thoughtless monster, completely losing his dignity and self-control.

We were always fearful when he was due back from tour. We knew the routine well. We knew what would happen. Mother would say, "Daddy is very tired. Now for goodness sake, don't upset him. He's had a very hard time. Behave yourselves!"

Father would come in and after a shower he would head straight for the pantry, the place where he stored the drinks, the cheap, local brew. On these occasions it seems, my father will have been transformed into some kind of demon over which he had no control. He would sit at the dining table, a bottle and glass before him, apparently unaware of where he was or what he was doing. A spell of heavy drinking would continue until dinner time. By the time the family gathered round the table, we were all scared of what might happen next. We kept silent. On mother's face a terrified look, pleading with him not to drink too much. Her pleas and protests would go unheeded; he simply brushed her aside.

On most occasions Richard would be his main target. Without knowing the reason, Richard got a sharp whack across his ear. "Let me see your hands," he would shout. "They are filthy. Go and wash them now! You should know better than to come to the table with grimy hands. And wash your grubby face as well!" This would be followed by a further blow to his head. Mother tried to suppress a slight cough from a piece of food getting stuck in her throat, almost in tears. All of us were terrified of what he might do next, who might get the next blow. We would sit quietly eating our food, trying not to move a muscle, with eyes fixed on our plates. Later, much later, we would be dismissed from the table and told to go to bed. At times like this, even Nath felt nervous removing the plates and clearing the table.

Some time during the night we would be woken suddenly by the terrifying sound of shattering glass. Helen and I would lie in terror as we tried to cover our ears against the noise of swearing, as did Blanche and Richard. There was nothing we could do but remain quiet in bed, out of harm's way. Father will simply have punched his fist across all the glassware on the sideboard, broken crockery and all mother's little ornaments now scattered all over the floor. Poor mother. It was no wonder she kept to her bed the following day, sick at heart, sad and helpless.

There would be an unnatural atmosphere the morning after one of these bouts. We crept about quietly in hushed silence. Mother in bed, father sitting at the breakfast table, silent. Was he perhaps shocked at the damage he had done? Was he concerned at the consternation on mother's face? Her deep hurt? Did he notice the fear on our faces? Was he aware of his crazed, wicked behaviour?

By late morning, father was usually back to his 'normal' self. He would try to make amends. He would go out and buy a whole new range of china and glassware; no expense spared. He would remain sober and uncommunicative for the next few days, maybe regretful for the havoc and distress he had caused. Maybe.

But this pattern of events was repeated almost every time he returned from tour. Out with the bottle and, by dinner time, Richard would get an undeserved punch or two, or more. Why was father so out of control in his dealings with Richard? We could not understand why he suddenly got his ears boxed for no apparent reason at the dinner table and so often beaten for some slight misdemeanour. Mother tried hard to answer our questions, often defending father's actions and making excuses for his frightful behaviour. "Your father has a very difficult job to do, he has a lot to contend with," she said on one occasion. "You must realise he needs to drink to forget his worries and it is the drink that causes him to behave in the way he does.

He doesn't really mean to be so frightening and destructive. He is a good man."

But a few months later, when father returned from one of his tours, he was in a particularly foul mood and began ranting and raving at Richard and beat him mercilessly for no reason. He shouted and swore at him, saying he was disobedient, undisciplined and thoroughly out of control, the cause of all our problems. "A thoroughly bad lot! Damn you!" he raged. He ordered him out of the house, saying, "It's high time you were out of here, you are old enough to fend for yourself – I don't ever want you back again! Get out of this house, I never want to see you again! Damn you, get out!"

Poor Richard. What had he done to deserve this?

Later, when father had calmed down a bit, mother pleaded with him, tried to reason with him, but father was adamant. He insisted that Richard leave home and learn to cope with life in the real world. Nor was his name to be mentioned in the household.

Mother was beside herself, helpless, in floods of tears. We were so scared of what might happen to him. We were extremely worried that he would not come back. We knew of no friends living nearby whom he could ask for help or shelter. Neither mother nor any of us children could face the future in the knowledge that Richard might be somewhere out there, wandering the streets among coolies and beggars.

It was Nath who came to the rescue. He moved some of his own belongings out from one of the servants' outhouses at the bottom of the garden and it was there that

Richard took shelter, in a dark room with a tiny window, locking the door so that father would not find him. We prayed father would not order the servants to search the garden, the hen house or the outhouses. It was a very tense time for all the family, for father's dark mood continued for several days.

The banishment of Richard lasted seven long days. Nath took care of him and made him as comfortable as he could, but we felt this was a very harsh, undeserved punishment. What could he have done to deserve this? Mother was ill with worry and took to her bed. The pain that this latest trauma caused her was plain to see. She wept quietly and could not be consoled. Nor was she able to keep down any food except for a few sips of water.

By the end of the week father grew concerned at her condition and Richard was allowed back in the house, browbeaten and even more frightened than before.

Richard Leaves Home

It was soon after this incident that Richard felt he must plan his future away from home. Because he had developed a talent for woodwork and furniture-making, he went to several firms dealing in carpentry and timber, but, because of the political uncertainty and the fact that he was considered a 'foreigner' in these parts, the job market for an unqualified youth like Richard was practically nil. He reckoned he would stand a better chance of an apprenticeship if he returned to India. But funds were tight. His interest in woodwork made no profit here; it was more of a hobby. He asked father for help towards his travel costs to India, but father refused point blank.

Mother suggested he write to Eugene whom she was sure would advise him in his search for work. Richard did as mother said; he told Eugene of recent events and begged Eugene to help him find a job in India. Richard also asked him to help fund his travel costs. Although Eugene was not exactly flush with money, he agreed to help Richard and within weeks sent Richard sufficient money to cover the journey, but only just. He explained it was all he could afford. Eugene had worked out a precise itinerary for his journey to Deolali (near Bombay), where Eugene was now stationed. He was to book his a passage by sea from Rangoon to Calcutta in advance. He was to find his way to the correct railway station where he was to board a specific train at the junctions given. It had all been worked out precisely in every detail. He was being entrusted with this money and needed to make it cover the entire journey. He was to use his own initiative, taking care not to run out of funds. He was to travel by the cheapest means possible. Eugene told him to be vigilant at all times. "Beware of thieves and pickpockets," he warned. "If you lose this money or have it stolen, then God help you!"

Richard was just sixteen and had never been away from home. He was trusting and straightforward, guileless perhaps. For the first time in his life, he would be entirely alone among some of the most unscrupulous pickpockets and fraudsters. Mother was extremely concerned that he was leaving with so little money to spare and pleaded with father many times to help towards his travelling expenses, but father refused, saying it would do Richard good to learn what life was all about in the tough world outside.

We were all desperately sorry to see Richard leave. All he took was a small bag containing a change of clothes and a bar of soap.

India is ridden with gangs of robbers and bandits, most of whom would not hesitate in killing a lone youth for a few pice. When you consider the vastness of India and Burma, it was no mean feat for a sixteen-year-old who had never left home before. But our prayers were answered and Richard finally arrived at his intended destination, Deolali. It had taken nearly five weeks of travel for him to meet up with Eugene, and he arrived exhausted, hungry and broke.

Eugene was well aware of mother's worries and misgivings about this journey and lost no time in letting her know that he had arrived safe and well.

Eugene accompanied Richard to several local firms in Bombay, arranging interviews and making numerous enquiries of friends and colleagues. He followed up every lead to find some kind of employment or apprenticeship scheme, but jobs were very difficult in the employment market for young men without qualifications. However, he had one more lead. A friend he had known in his youth, now a successful engineer, was his last hope. Ashley Mann, who worked in Howrah, near Calcutta, replied to Eugene's enquiry saying he would try to find Richard a job in the engineering company where he was presently employed. Ashley met with Richard but no job resulted from this meeting. After several weeks, and being unable to support Richard on his military pay, he had to admit defeat and send him back home to Monywa.

And so it was that a despondent and dispirited Richard reluctantly boarded a ship in Calcutta to take him to Rangoon, back to his cheerless life in Monywa to face a sometimes drunk and violent father.

Mother wept when she saw his thin, gaunt face, the look of hopelessness and despair on his face. He never told of the hardship he surely would have experienced on this journey, but we girls were overjoyed to see him back – we had missed him so. We tried to cheer him up but, sadly for us all, father's attitude towards him deteriorated further as poor Richard continued to be the butt of his frustrations.

However, as events were later to unfold, this unsuccessful adventure which Richard had undertaken across the great expanse of India, was to stand Blanche, Helen and myself in good stead, for our survival was to depend on the shrewdness, cunning and trickery he had learnt and the difficulties he had overcome during this seemingly fruitless journey.

Above: Father (second from right), with colleagues from the Post & Telegraphs Department at Monywa. The photograph is undated but was probably taken in June 1940.

4

War Comes to Burma

Burma and India formed part of a vast British Empire upon which it was said the sun never set. These countries, just two of many, had been under British rule for over four hundred years. Now the political landscape was changing. The people were getting restless and their leaders were pressing for more power and control over their own destinies and demanding independence from Britain.

Here in Monywa, father and mother would often comment on the world news as we listened to debates taking place in Delhi and London. Father explained that, besides the sporadic rioting in India and Burma in the cause of independence, on the other side of the world, in distant lands to the west, Germany had been at war with Britain for over two years. German forces were gaining the upper hand, inflicting huge losses on the British. They had already occupied Poland and the Netherlands, killing and torturing hundreds of people as they overran northern Europe. At the same time British forces were trying to defend their territory in North Africa and suffering setbacks on the high seas as

German U-boats attacked shipping in the Atlantic and the Indian Ocean. It would appear that Britain was fighting the enemy on all fronts. The world news was becoming ever more disturbing by the day.

Fierce battles were also being fought in south-east Asia. The Japanese were long-standing enemies of China and had been at war with them for a number of years. China had always been a target of Japanese ambition and, when in the 1930s Japan seized Manchuria in a most terrible, brutal war, the conquest of the Chinese republic seemed virtually within their sight. Then in 1937, a full-scale war started when Japan attacked Peking. By June 1941, she held all the supply routes that connected China to the rest of the world, with the exception of the Burma Road at the northern tip of Burma. In order to put a stop to the flow of tons of American war material being transported into China through the Burma Road, this area became the focus of attention for the Japanese army.

It was also said that the purpose of the invasion by the Japanese in south-east Asia was to acquire the natural resources of oil, rubber, rice, tungsten and teak in which Borneo, Java, Sumatra, Malaya and Burma were rich. Without these, Japan could not carry on its planned domination of the area. There were reports of the rapid progress of the Japanese army and, within months, there was talk of war.

Father said he could not believe that the Japanese were attacking and conquering these lands so rapidly and with such apparent ease. He explained that danger for us would come from the east. He spread out a large map of the world on the floor and pointed to Japan. It looked small and insignificant compared to the huge landmass that formed south-east Asia but he said that, judging from news reports of Japanese infiltration, nearly all this region, including Hong Kong and Malaya, could soon be under Japanese occupation. The situation looked exceedingly grim.

It was soon after this that our former landlord, Mr Wong, called to tell us of his family's anxiety at the worsening situation. He said they had reluctantly come to the decision to return to their homeland. They felt that, if the Japanese succeeded in invading Burma, they could find themselves trapped with no hope of escape. He reiterated the fact that Japan had been at war with China since 1930 when they invaded Manchuria, causing the death of tens of thousands of innocent civilians. He said he knew of several Chinese families living in Burma who feared for their lives at the progress of the Japanese invading forces and were now leaving the country to return to China.

It was with sadness that we said goodbye to our old landlord, his wife and our playmates. They had been good friends and caring neighbours during our stay in our previous home.

Mother spoke often of her fears, of what our family might do should it become necessary for us to leave here and return to India, but father was quick to dismiss the idea. He held a responsible government post as head of the Post & Telegraphs Department in Monywa. There was no question of us leaving, we would be safe here, having the full support of the government. We must stay calm, stand firm and not be caught up in rumour. We carry on as normal, he insisted.

But not many days passed before we heard that Japanese Imperial Forces had overrun the Philippines, attacked Australia and New Guinea, and now occupied Borneo, Thailand, Singapore, Malaya, Indochina and the oil fields of the Dutch East Indies. Before very long, they were pouring over the Thai border into Burma – the last unoccupied nation in south-east Asia, the sole buffer between India, and the source of China's last artery of outside supply, the Burma Road.

As we listened to the radio we heard that 370 Japanese planes from six aircraft carriers had attacked the United States' Pacific fleet at Pearl Harbour, which adjoins Honolulu, severely damaging two U.S. battleships. They had also sunk a number of American ships moored in the harbour, temporarily extinguishing the U.S. Pacific fleet, which resulted in the United States declaring war on Japan.

Almost every evening as we listened to the World Service of the BBC, father would chart out on the map the progress the Japanese forces were making. Each week they were gaining territory. They were now almost on the doorstep of Malaya. It didn't look very far from where we were and, as the days went by, both father and mother became increasingly worried. We noticed mother had started to do strange things. She spent long hours counting the cutlery, the linen, the clothes pegs; repeatedly cleaning and dusting, re-arranging ornaments and rugs and generally being unnaturally fastidious about every minute detail. She also wanted us to be within her sight at all times. It was as if she was trying to distract her mind from what was happening in the world outside which she could not control, to things within the home that she could.

Each day, my parents listened with growing concern to the world news, especially of the rapid Japanese advance towards us here in Burma, but father also expressed his puzzlement at how the British military and naval authorities had appeared so unprepared for the war in Europe. Would they then have the resources and manpower to defend us here against the Japanese should we become embroiled in a war in this part of the world?

But unknown to us, for it was known only to those in command, in the first week of December 1941, the Japanese landed 26,000 troops on the strip of land that joins Malaya and Thailand. Half the invaders went south to take Singapore, the other half went north to occupy Thailand, and within a week another column, guided by the Burmese Liberation Army, pushed westwards into Burma. With the fall of Java, they now turned their full attention to Burma.

The Japanese technique of invasion was elaborately prepared and efficiently executed. For invasion from the sea, they chose to land on beaches which had been reconnoitred from the air and by secret agents on the ground. They usually landed just before dawn during rainy or stormy weather. The Japanese were similar in looks and stature to the Burmese, and disguised in native dress were able to filter through British defence lines undetected.

With each passing week there were more rumours of

the rapid progress of the Japanese army. We heard reports of fierce battles being fought in the southern area of Burma near its border with Thailand. In spite of this, up to December 1941 when America entered the war, the military had regarded the likelihood of invasion as remote, so it was not surprising that the civil government did not take comprehensive measures to educate and prepare people for it.

Nonetheless, people were getting restless and impatient for some direction from the ruling authorities as to how they were to prepare themselves in case of attack. This eventually came in a special broadcast given by the Governor, Sir Reginald Dorman-Smith from his headquarters in Rangoon. He tried to allay people's fears by assuring them that the British government was prepared for any attack the Japanese might make. He stressed that there was no need for them to take any drastic action. The situation was under control. Every working citizen was to remain at his post and carry out his duties as normal. However, within a few weeks of the broadcast, on 23rd December 1941, a large force of Japanese aircraft attacked the main port of Rangoon and brought it almost to a standstill.

Earlier in the war Japanese troops, headed by elephant-riding Thais, had filtered through jungle trails from Thailand and cut off the lower strip of Burma with its important air bases. They advanced across the muddy Sittang River flats to circle Rangoon. Several hundred crated American trucks, cars and jeeps on the quays were destroyed by order of the British Army. Wharves, warehouses, storage tanks and vast supplies of rice were set alight to stop them falling into the hands of the enemy.

Many Burmese revolutionaries, who had long yearned to be free of British rule, now helped the Japanese landing parties. Hundreds of unarmed Britons and ordinary civilians were killed in the streets of Rangoon and elsewhere by these rebels.

On Boxing Day 1941, we heard a report that 60 Japanese bombers had devastated some areas of Rangoon on Christmas morning. Over two thousand people had died in the streets, most of them killed as they stood watching in horror and disbelief as bombs fell from the sky. Terrified people were abandoning their homes and possessions and streaming out of Rangoon by any means available: by train, by bus or on bullock-carts. A few families were fortunate enough to board the last overcrowded ships leaving Rangoon, bound for Calcutta.

As the invasion had started in the south, the only way to escape the bombardment of Rangoon was to flee up country. The British authorities were now forced into making arrangements for the needs of refugees driven northwards.

A plan was hastily prepared for the evacuation of foreign nationals wishing to leave. A route was mapped out through the rugged and mountainous region of the north, which was to lead to the border with India. Paths were cleared through the dense forests and temporary huts were constructed out of wood and thatch for night shelter along the way. Since the first part of the proposed evacuation north was by river, riverboats and other river craft were requisitioned. Basic food supplies and medical teams were organised and put in place throughout the route for the expected influx of refugees from the south. Gurkha soldiers were deployed to escort and protect them.

Our little town, with its strategic location on the banks of the River Chindwin, was selected as a staging post for people arriving from the southern regions of Burma and, quite suddenly, Monywa became an important junction where, for many of the refugees, the train journey terminated. After an overnight stop, they would continue their journey towards the Indian border either by truck, steamboat, ferry, or any other river craft they could acquire.

At first there was just a trickle of people passing through our little town. But within a couple of weeks, our local railway station was inundated with men, women and children crowding into the waiting room, some sleeping on rugs on the crowded platform, others spilling out on to the dusty streets, clutching their few belongings. All were in desperate need of shelter.

After discussing the tragic circumstances of these people with mother, father felt we should help in some small way. Mother agreed that we could at least offer them a meal and a bed, or even a mattress on the floor for the night. So it became a daily routine for father to go to the railway station every evening to bring home a couple of families with small children who were travelling on their own, their menfolk presumably having to be left behind at their posts.

These families would often tell horrendous stories of the chaotic situation in the cities, and the looting and wanton destruction by the Burmese themselves. They told of the despair of some people at having to leave behind their homes and possessions. But most of all, they feared for their children.

Father said these were desperate, uncertain times. He grew worried that, although he had on a number of occasions asked for direction as to what he should do with regard to our own family, there was still no proper response from his superiors. He was told that he must wait for explicit instructions. Now he worried that we could find ourselves in a somewhat similar predicament to these displaced people and, although we had been advised to keep calm, not to make hasty decisions or take unnecessary risks, the true situation, gathered from the stories these folk told, was serious indeed. He hoped that should we ever find ourselves in a similar plight and become homeless, the hospitality and goodwill we extend to these unfortunate people would be repaid – a hundredfold. We were to recall his words many times, as events were later to unfold.

Above:. President Franklin D. Roosevelt said that the Japanese attack on Pearl Harbour would "live for ever in the annals of infamy". This photograph, portraying just a fraction of the damage, was taken on 7 December 1941 by a sailor serving on USS Quapaw (ATF-110) but not developed until 2009, having spent 68 years in a Brownie camera stored in a foot locker.

5

Leaving Home

These were hectic and worrying times. The world outside seemed to be in a state of utter turmoil and uncertainty. Many of the families stopping with us every night spoke of the indiscriminate bombing of towns and villages, the capturing and killing of innocent people, of chaos and confusion and the breakdown of law and order. Here in Monywa, we heard of increasing incidents of disturbance and disorder. Besides, the town was full of refugees milling about, doing their final shopping for their journey north.

Father was now supervising the digging of an air-raid shelter in our back garden and equipping it with tinned food – corned beef, sardines, beans, dried milk, cheese and other necessities. Sleeping bunks were erected; a small radio, Kerosene oil for lanterns and a primus stove were also bought and stored in a large trunk in the shelter. Mother was in a constant state of anxiety and, if any of us were out of her sight for a moment, she would get into a state of panic and call out until she got an answer to say we were all right.

Father became restless and frustrated as the days

went by, for it was obvious to him that the invaders were closing in, apparently meeting little or no resistance. There was no comment or acknowledgement from his superiors. No orders or suggestions as to what he might do about his employees or family were yet forthcoming, in spite of his many requests for evacuation plans. Because of the nature of his job, he realised that until he received definitive orders he was obliged to stay at his post. But now he decided the time had come to take matters into his own hands and make plans to secure the safety of his own family – my mother and us four children.

He was greatly troubled about mother's deteriorating condition. She had been suffering ill health off and on for a number of years. With recent preparations for safety and changes happening in our own garden she was getting ever more worried and fretful. He realised that she was in no fit state to face the rigours of a journey through dense jungle that was likely to be worse than anything he had experienced on his tours. He could not contemplate her walking through the rough mountainous track or being able to cope with the many hazards she might encounter on the way. He knew she could not survive without a constant and reliable companion to assist her. Trekking with a group of people in her present state of health was out of the question. He would need to get her to safety by some other means.

However, we children were fit enough to make the journey with the help of Nath who was happy to accompany us. He would also send Banasidas, a tough, muscular man who for many years had been in his employ and had accompanied him on numerous tours and who was familiar with the terrain. Both men were loyal, dependable and honest. He pondered long and hard about the few options that were still open to him. Time was running out.

After much soul searching and debate with his colleagues, he decided that Richard, Blanche, Helen and I would join a convoy of people leaving within the next few days. He would need to inform his superiors and send a telegram to his sister Agnes in Lahore, asking her to take us in for few weeks, explaining his fears and the urgency of our situation.

Trying to convince mother that it was imperative for us children to leave without her was one of father's most difficult tasks. He assured her that it was in our best interests to leave as soon as possible, adding that she was not fit enough to accompany us, but that they would both follow together on the same journey in a few weeks' time. He promised that we would be safe. He would send two of his most trusted men to be our personal bodyguards – Nath and Banasidas.

"The news today is not good," father said. "It could get worse in the coming weeks. The children will be safe, dear. They will be in the care of an officially organised squad of soldiers, and bona fide officials will protect them along the route until they reach their destination in India. Nath will be with them throughout the journey but Banasidas will have to return when the children reach Mawlaik where British officials will take over their care." Father emphasised the importance of us leaving as soon as arrangements could be made, possibly in the next few days. He reminded her of the many families who a few weeks ago had spent the night with us and were now safe with their families in India.

"I'm sure Agnes and Alice will take them in until we get to Lahore. I can send them a telegram to expect the children," father assured her. "When I receive confirmation of their itinerary, I will also ask Eugene, May and Tom to meet them somewhere along the way and ask them to accompany them to Agnes's home."

Initially my father had expected to return to Lahore after a four-year tour of duty in Burma and, since his two sisters resided there, it seemed the obvious choice for our destination. Although he had not been in touch with them for a number of years because of a petty quarrel, he felt certain they would take us in until he and mother returned to India.

Mother was in great distress at the thought of us leaving without her or father, but she fully understood father's logic and agreed that we should join the next group of people on condition that they both follow within days of our leaving. Father tried to reassure her, but she was heartbroken at the thought of us losing our way or being kidnapped, or having bombs dropped on us, for did she not hear stories of this kind every day? She started to go through our clothes, selecting the best and placing them lovingly into a small case. She wept silently as she hugged us in turn. We would all need substantial shoes. She would take us to the bazaar the next morning and buy us each a new pair. But father said, "No dear, they will have to make do with what they are wearing. There is no time to do any shopping."

At this time, the shopping area was chaotic. The stone-throwing, looting and petty feuds between Indian shopkeepers and the local Burmese was getting worse. Most of the Chinese traders and many of the Indian shopkeepers had closed down and left already for China or India. It was not safe to go anywhere, father said, least of all to the bazaar.

Arrangements were being made hurriedly once the decision was made for us to leave, and the following day father and Nath packed a small case with delicacies for the journey: tinned Kraft cheese, sardines, sausages, corned beef, beans, biscuits and sweets, which were a very rare treat for us. This case containing all our goodies turned out to be quite heavy. Father said there was sufficient food here to see us through the trip, which he reckoned would take about two weeks. He assured us that government officials would meet us at the Indian border to advise and help us with the onward journey.

The painting of mother and father that hung in the sitting room just fitted into the second case. So too did a few family photos, a silver teapot and some cut glass dishes edged with silver, while other small personal possessions that had been in the family for years were carefully packed amongst our clothes.

Mother packed a few toiletries and fruit for our immediate needs into a small basket, called a "parr". Into a soft 'Shan' shoulder bag, father placed a packet of papers relating to his employment in the Post & Telegraphs Department, his personal insurance and documents to do with financial matters. He also put into the same shoulder bag a purse of newly minted coins, thinking perhaps that if the Japanese printed their own paper money (which they later did), coins would be more acceptable as legal tender; paper notes could lose their value. He also put in the medals he had been awarded for service in the First World War.

Richard, now aged eighteen, had been a great asset to mother in helping her with the various tasks involved in having visitors every night. He was proving quite a hit by keeping them amused and acting the clown. Father was not drinking so much these days, and was more amenable and tolerant towards us. Also, of late, his attitude towards Richard had softened considerably, for Richard tried hard to please him but still remained afraid.

It was on the evening before our departure that father took Richard aside. "Son," he said, "now that you've proved to be a more responsible adult, I'm depending on you to take care of your sisters. I know you are capable. There may be many difficulties ahead of you, but I expect you to look to their welfare and make any decisions in their best interests. You will get help from government sponsored officials along the way but you will still need to protect them throughout the journey until you arrive at your Aunt Agnes's home in Lahore. She will be expecting you. Her address is with the papers in Blanche's bag. Helen will need help if the going gets tough; she may need to be carried but you won't be alone, you'll have Nath and Banasidas to help. Maude might also need your support sometimes. Take care of Blanche and yourself too. Try never to be parted along the way; remain close together always and guard them with your life".

He repeated his instruction to Blanche that on no account was she to be parted from this bag. He said finally, "These are important papers that prove your identity. Keep the bag with you at all times. Whatever you do, do not lose it. Take care of yourself and of one another." With tears in his eyes, father hugged us, saying that he and mother would soon be joining us at some point on our journey. He added, "All being well, we will be following you in a couple of days or weeks, and, God willing, will meet you at Aunt Agnes's home, if not before. This war will not last forever. The bloody Japs will be stopped and defeated sooner or later. All of you, take care and God speed."

The heart-rending day arrived early next morning when we had to say goodbye to mother. Father said she had had a very restless night. That morning, she looked pale and tired. Her thoughts were plain to see. It seemed only weeks ago we were an ordinary family living our lives peaceably, quietly enjoying our daily pleasures and working out our little problems. Now, suddenly, all was chaos and confusion. The whole place indoors was in disarray, the contents of drawers spewed out all over the floor in our effort to try to find some valuable piece to fit into any small space in our cases. And outside, in place of fruit trees and a duck pond, there was a newly dug, ugly air-raid shelter covered in dusty soil.

I'm sure mother had tried to blot out the many

unbelievable stories told by visiting families of Japanese cruelty, of dead bodies lying in the streets unburied, of babies being snatched from the arms of mothers and brutally killed in front of them. Now her own family was being torn apart, her own children leaving to make a journey through uncharted jungle. What terrors might they have to face on the way? The tears mother shed that day ran until she could cry no more. She could not be comforted. We knew her heart was bleeding too.

A Sad Parting

Father had told us to be brave and strong; he wanted no tears. It was difficult for us to be brave when we saw the distressed state mother was in; she looked heartbroken, too upset to accompany us to the river. Father said we were to say our goodbyes now, remembering that we would meet up again within the next few days. He said we must not linger, we needed to hurry to catch the steamboat in good time – to stay any longer would simply prolong the pain of parting. So it was that we hugged and kissed mother hurriedly, saying we would see her soon.

Father, Richard, Blanche, Helen and I, along with Nath and Banasidas carrying our cases, climbed into the two waiting tongas and slowly made the short trip down to the little mooring, where we caught our first glimpse of the boat. It looked smaller than we imagined and was tied to a post on the river alongside a few other similar craft. I cannot remember its name but it looked rather forlorn and silent, as if it was going nowhere. As we approached, we could hear men's voices and the sound of knocking. There were a couple of men working on deck and a rather unsafe gangplank was in place. A number of people who were to be our companions on the journey were gathering with their baggage waiting a short distance away for instructions to board. There were no signs of any official escorts.

The steamboat was scheduled to leave at 10.30 am, by which time about fifty people had gathered round. A few children were getting restless as we waited in the blazing sun until it was past midday. Then father went over and shouted to a man who appeared on board, "Why are we all being kept waiting for so long? What's the trouble? Who's in charge around here?" A fat little Chinese man emerged from inside. He had a bald head, a round face, a flat nose, with mean hostile slit eyes under black bushy eyebrows. He shouted back officiously, "I am the captain. You do not catch the steamboat today. I already told Mr Major. You go home. The boat no working, out of action. The engine need repair. We make it safe. The river very high upstream. Come back tomorrow, all of you, same time."

Reluctantly the crowd dispersed. Father was furious that no one had informed us of the change of plan. There was no alternative but to return home. By the time we got back father was soaked in perspiration. He was hot and exasperated. Time was crucial to our safety, delay would only mean postponing the inevitable. He said he just hoped we would not be delayed for more than twenty-four hours.

We were so pleased to see mother again. She, on her part, was most surprised to see us; we were back together again under her wing. It might even have crossed her mind for a moment that the nightmare was over. A fleeting smile of joy lit up her face. But, of course, father had to bring her down to earth. He explained the reason for the delay and said, "We'll have to come to terms with the inevitable and let the children leave while it is still possible for them to be escorted in safety, dear. They will have to leave tomorrow. We must be prepared. It is for their good and ours. There is no other option. The longer we delay their departure, the harder it will be for them to make the journey and even more painful for us to let them go."

Father told us that night that we would have to leave very early the following morning and be as quiet as we could. Mother was not to be disturbed; she could not be put through another harrowing parting. It was father who woke us before dawn the following morning. Nath had already prepared our breakfast; Banasidas had eaten and was waiting downstairs with our cases.

Mother was still in her bedroom. When we were ready to leave, father would not allow us to see her. But the door to her room was slightly ajar. I told myself: of course we would be together again, and soon. Perhaps in a week or two at the most, as father had said. So why was I now suddenly gripped with fear that this might be the last time I saw her? I peeped in and caught a glimpse of her.

Mother was kneeling by her bed, rapt in prayer. I filled my heart and soul with her image. I see her still.

6

Escape from Burma

We spotted our boat long before we arrived at the muddy river. It looked much too small to accommodate the large crowd of people waiting now to board her. We heard the Chinese captain shouting loudly some distance away, flailing his arms about in an argument with a man attempting to take a bicycle aboard.

A crew member and a man in army uniform sat at a small table taking down the names of passengers as they filtered through on to the boat. A few Gurkha soldiers dressed in khaki uniforms carrying rifles were helping the very young, old and infirm up the gangplank with their belongings.

Soon father was giving us each a tight hug, emphasising his instructions to always stay close together. "You are to be brave and face the journey courageously. You must help each other and, whatever happens, on no account must you get separated," he repeated. Father promised we would not be on our own for long, since he was already making plans for himself and mother to follow very soon.

We then boarded the crowded boat with Nath and Banasidas close behind. Richard, eighteen years of age now, said we were not to be afraid. This was going to be fun, a great adventure. Just what he had been reading about in his 'Eagle' comic.

When we reached the army officer at the point of boarding, Richard gave our names and other details with a certain degree of self-confidence. It didn't seem long, with all the hustle and bustle of the crowd with their belongings, before we found ourselves clinging to the handrails of the boat, watching father standing on the mud flats waving goodbye as the crew cast off from the small makeshift pier. We stayed close to Richard as we left the shore and continued to wave to father as he slowly faded into the distance, trying hard to hold back the tears. But when we were alone in the middle of the wide river, surrounded on all sides by strangers, staring at father's receding figure on the bank, I was overwhelmed by such a feeling of desolation that I wanted almost to jump overboard and swim back to him and stay home with mother.

The boat then swung round, groaning with weight, and all too soon we lost sight of father. Richard quickly wiped away his tears and unhesitatingly took control, clasping Helen's hand, and found us seats in the tightly packed boat. From this moment on, we were dependent on him for everything. Quite suddenly, it seemed, he had grown to full manhood and revealed his true character as a responsible and mature adult.

We were in the middle of the river, with father

barely out of sight, when the captain announced, loudly and authoritatively, that all provisions being carried by passengers would have to be left on board. He emphasised that he would allow no food, be it fresh, tinned or preserved, to be consumed on board or taken ashore at the point of disembarkation. He said that simple meals would be provided. "The food left by you is earmarked for refugees expected to follow later when government stocks are likely to be depleted," he said. "The journey you are about to undertake now has been organised by the British authorities and all your needs will be met along the route. There will be no need for anyone to carry surplus foodstuff in their baggage."

Richard and Blanche looked at each other in dismay. "How the hell can he do this? It can't be right," they whispered. Father had warned us to be careful about what we ate at the rest camps, adding that hygiene would not be high on the list of priorities in places such as these where so many people had to be catered for. Food would most likely be rationed. He said elephants might be the only form of transport as we travelled further north into the mountains, and did not think it would harm anybody to carry what food they could. On the contrary, it might be to the advantage of all. Now we've got to give it up! Can't we keep some of it back?

But Richard decided it was in our best interests to obey the captain's orders, he was deadly serious. We were under his command, at his mercy. We felt vulnerable and dared not hide even a couple of tins of sardines in our pockets for fear of being caught and risk being ejected from the boat. Richard whispered to Nath and Banasidas, saying there was nothing we could do but hand over the case containing our food. We were not the only ones to leave our goodies behind; many other frightened people on board the steamboat that night who were carrying a few provisions had to leave them to the fat, avaricious captain.

The steamboat was not designed to carry more than about thirty people, but here we were, perhaps fifty, packed closely together, hardly able to move.

In the early days of the evacuation process, the authorities had thought it necessary to send convoys of Indians, and those Burmese wishing to leave, in separate ethnic groups and by different routes because of their different language, culture and the recent clashes between Muslims and Hindus. Now people of all denominations were quite literally in the same boat and were all making the same journey together, sharing the same space, camps and shelters. No segregation here: Europeans, British, Eurasians, Indians and a few Burmese. This group was from various parts of Burma, all thankful to be aboard – all in search of a safe place ahead of the advancing Japanese Imperial Forces.

The River Chindwin is a tributary of the Irrawaddy. It runs through green and fertile land. It is also home to scorpion fish, poisonous sea snakes and crocodiles, some of which grow to nine feet. The dense green is broken by numerous sandbanks which seem to change position from day to day and hour to hour, depending on the speed of the current, as the banks are formed by the shifting silt. The river widens in places becoming slow and calm and, on that first day, we crawled along as the heavy boat struggled upstream, but as we continued along, the river narrowed and after a while it started to flow swiftly, becoming turbulent at times, causing the boat to lurch as it rolled through small rapids. When we passed the village of Kani that evening, the river was quite high, lapping under the many small wooden dwellings we passed built on stilts.

On that first night and the two that followed, we were sometimes terrified by the sound of the swirling current. In the darkness we could hear the occasional rush of water as we clung to each other. We were uncomfortable and tired as we sat there, watching the dark forest and occasionally passing wooden houses along the way. We were fed on chappaties with a spoonful of dhal. Drinking water was poured into our cupped hands, most of it spilling on to the deck. During the night we dozed off on the hard, uncomfortable seats. Helen was seven years old now but still missing and whimpering for mother. She did not fully realise that mother was not with us and that we had left her behind. She clutched her teddy bear, and Blanche and I tried to comfort and reassure her that mother would soon be joining us.

During the second night on board, our courage seemed to desert us, for apart from the physical discomfort of the hard bench, we were plagued by vicious mosquitoes. Other creepy crawlies caused considerable itching and scratching. We were surrounded by the eerie sounds of animals, while strange noises from the dense growth kept us awake. The humid heat and odour of so many people in such a small space unable to wash properly was becoming ever more uncomfortable. Many of our fellow passengers were suffering in the same way. From time to time, Nath and Banasidas fetched us water to refresh our hands and faces. Blanche used her handkerchief, which she moistened with water to wipe our faces.

We spoke in whispers and wondered what lay ahead and what other conditions the nasty captain would impose upon us on some sudden whim. He was a bumptious little man who kept shouting orders in Burmese, flailing his arms about, to crew and passengers alike as though he were herding animals. We tried to ignore the noise he made and kept to ourselves. On one occasion, he tried to snatch a ring from one of the women, telling her that he would keep it safe while she was aboard. The woman refused most emphatically, so he ordered her and her daughter to go to the rear end of the boat where the latrines were located. Besides the valuable ruby ring, she was also wearing several gold bangles that had caught the captain's eye, which she had bought from the proceeds of the sale of her house and which she intended converting to cash to fund her new life in India.

We were into our second day on board when we heard the distant sound of aeroplanes. All eyes were raised to the sky, fearing that, if it was enemy aircraft, they could blow us out of the boat, for we were clearly visible from above at this point. The captain signalled us with his arms from the far end, indicating that we should squat and keep low on the deck. Our only protection was the benches we were sitting on. Although the boat was packed with people, we managed to crouch down under the benches while the crew attempted to adjust some awnings in an effort perhaps to hide some of us. Three aircraft approached, then turned and swooped low overhead. The captain said they were Japanese fighters. They must have seen us, he said. We heard from others in the boat that they might be spotter planes. Someone speculated that they had probably spent their bombs already. Thankfully, to the relief of us all, they turned again and continued on their original course.

As we continued our journey up river we were scared that Japanese troops might already be ahead of us, creeping in the undergrowth. Richard told us not to worry as he pointed out a crew member carrying binoculars and a solitary Gurkha soldier carrying a rifle. We wondered if there were any guns on board if we should need to defend ourselves in the event of an attack.

After this incident with the aircraft, the boat kept near the water's edge, getting some cover from the tall trees and bamboo that grew close to the river's edge. All around we could hear the sound of birds, monkeys screeching high in the trees and other strange, frightening noises, especially at night.

We reached the small town of Mingin the next morning, where we were permitted to get off the boat for half an hour to stretch our legs and to take on stores and fresh water. We were told strictly to stay within sight of the boat. The following day we arrived at Kalewa where we spent a couple of hours.

I cannot remember how many days we had been on the boat, perhaps five or six, when the captain announced that we would soon be approaching our destination, the village of Mawlaik. We felt a great relief when the village came into view – a village of wooden huts built on stilts by the river's edge and, further inland, a row of more substantial houses where villagers were milling about, tending their chickens and livestock. There were men lopping trees and piling them up by the river. A number of elephants were working the logs. Some were tethered with huge baskets on their backs.

There was a cheerful chatter and murmurs of thankfulness from all the passengers as the boat pulled into Mawlaik. We had arrived at a small stretch of sandy beach along the riverside where ropes were tied to a temporary wooden landing stage and a few planks of wood placed on the boat for us to go ashore. We followed Richard closely down the gangplank. He carried the overnight bag containing a few clothes and toiletries. We were pleasantly surprised to discover that he had hidden a bag of sweets in with the toiletries. Nath followed close behind carrying two small cases and a small basket.

Sadly at this point, we had to say goodbye to Banasidas, for father had instructed him to return to Monywa after delivering us safely into the hands of the British authorities at Mawlaik; he was still officially employed by the Post & Telegraphs Department.

We had made the first leg of the journey safely and were greatly relieved to be delivered at last from the clutches of the vile, detestable captain.

In the clearing under a rough shelter, there were some officials and a few Gurkha soldiers studying papers and making notes at a table. There was already a queue of people waiting to give their details, after which they were being led to some houses nearby. It was hot, everyone was tired and there was a feeling of hostility because of bullying and shouting by officials when suddenly Helen started crying. "I want mummy, I want to go home," she kept repeating. Blanche and I tried to comfort and quieten her. We were so afraid of drawing attention to ourselves as we were the only family in the group not accompanied by either parent or guardian. Blanche was seventeen and I was a skinny, small, twelve-year-old. Richard said we should mingle with some older adults, hoping no one would notice we were travelling by ourselves. We could say Nath was accompanying us; the papers he carried showed he was in father's employ but not our guardian.

Above: Maude in April 1942 outside one of the refugees' shelters. This photograph shows clearly the rough-and-ready construction of these buildings, which were erected in haste to facilitate the safe passage of those fleeing to safety ahead of the Japanese invasion.

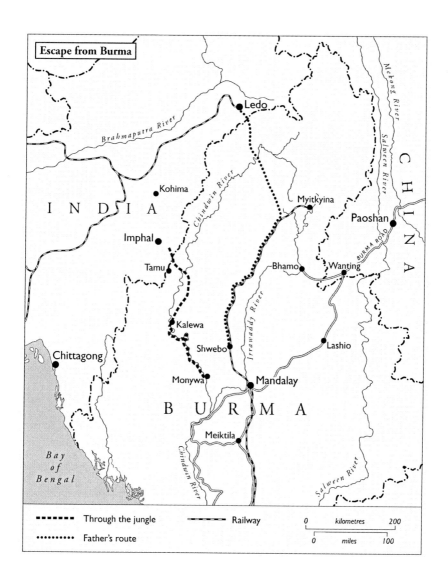

Escape from Burma

INDIA

CHINA

BURMA

Bay of Bengal

Brahmaputra River

Mekong River

Salween River

Chindwin River

Irrawaddy River

Chindwin River

Salween River

BURMA ROAD

Ledo

Kohima

Myitkyina

Paoshan

Imphal

Tamu

Bhamo

Wanting

Kalewa

Shwebo

Lashio

Chittagong

Monywa

Mandalay

Meiktila

- - - - - - Through the jungle   - = - = - Railway

· · · · · · · · Father's route

0   kilometres   200

0   miles   100

101

Above: The family's first home at Monywa, photographed in July 1938 – a time when life in Burma was becoming more unsettled due to the growing pressure for independence, which encouraged xenophobia. Members of the family can be seen on the first floor veranda.

7

Trekking Through the Jungle

The Nyenchentangla range of mountains in the north runs down from Tibet and China to where India meets the northernmost tip of Burma. This same range turns south, changing into the Patkai Hills. It makes a formidable natural barrier of rugged country. Here the vegetation is dense and entangles the jungle floor separating northern Burma from Assam in India. The dense growth is impenetrable in places. We had been warned at the outset that many wild animals roam the jungle freely – dogs, hyenas, wild boar, snakes and scorpions. A rough, narrow track which only pack animals could negotiate in the past had been widened and made safe by the authorities. This was the path that would lead us to India.

Now here we were, in a clearing by the river, part of a group of about 150 people, being directed towards three British army officers. They were dressed in khaki shirts and shorts, tough army boots and khaki pith helmets. A few Gurkha soldiers were instructing people to queue in an orderly way.

When we were gathered round the officers, one of them stood up and spoke to the crowd. He said he would be leading the way through the jungle; the journey would take approximately a week depending on weather conditions and the health and safety of the group. He went into some detail about what to expect. We were to start early the following morning.

We would be accompanied by five Gurkha soldiers from his regiment to act as guides and protect us from bandits, dacoits and wild animals. We were warned that nomads, familiar with every inch of this territory, were known to kill travellers who wandered unescorted into the jungle. He said we were to keep close together in one group and not split up from the main party. The strict timetable had to be adhered to. Only a limited number of people could be catered for at any one time at rest camps. New groups were expected each day and delays could cause a build-up and lead to a breakdown of the entire evacuation process. Coolies would accompany us on the journey to help those people who were unfortunate enough to fall ill or be injured.

Our schedule was explained to us as follows. We were to make an early start each day. Breakfast would be served from six in the morning and we were to assemble by seven-thirty for the next leg of the journey. We would be expected to walk approximately ten miles a day. On reaching rest camp at about three in the afternoon, we would be given refreshment consisting of a snack and a drink. After a wash down and a short rest, we would be provided with a simple meal in the evening and be allocated a sleeping bunk in huts along the way. The officer told us that fresh water would be carried by coolies, and that we were strictly forbidden to drink from streams along the way as the water was polluted, possibly poisoned, and on no account should we attempt to drink it. He said that there were streams located near some camps higher in the mountains where the water was known to be clean enough for drinking, which we would be told about. The water supplied in buckets at camps was specifically for washing purposes only. We were not to drink it. "Do not even wash your mouth with it", he warned.

The camps were not fenced off so, for the safety of all, a strict curfew was in force to stop people wandering into the jungle. "On no account are you to explore your surroundings. The jungle is full of hidden dangers and it is easy to lose one's bearings. Men cannot be spared to send out search parties. Those granted permission will be allowed to collect fresh water outside the camp but will have to return by five-thirty at the latest." The official added in a straightforward, unpretentious manner, "You will have to be aware of snakes, scorpions and other creatures like wild boar, bears and monkeys that swing from the tops of trees. Cross the streams with care as they are full of creatures that could give you a nasty, painful nip."

He then assured us that we would be looked after during the trip. "Every effort will be made to get you to the Indian border safely. Medical supplies are being carried and you will get help in case of injury or bites. In the eventuality of any serious medical problems, you will be attended to by an Army Medical Officer at each camp. We have a few coolies who will help the elderly and infirm with their luggage. You will of course be provided with rations at the rest camps."

After being dismissed by the officer, the group took off in an orderly manner towards a large clearing where there were rows of huts with thatched roofs, roughly woven thatch walls and mud floors, providing simple shelter for the night. Inside each section were four bunk bends. A durree, a lightly woven cotton blanket, covered each hammock-like bed. All the camps along the route were constructed in a similar way. They looked lightweight and fragile, obviously not built to withstand the monsoon.

That first evening, we were a bit apprehensive and kept very close to Richard for we knew no one in the group. We could rely only on the protection of faithful Nath who always remained close by. Richard made every attempt to cheer us up. He said, "Come on kids, this is going to be a great adventure. It's going to be fun. We're all fit and healthy. Ten miles a day? Nothing to it. It'll be a stroll, we'll manage it easy-peasy!"

Day One

The next morning, we were woken early by the sound of a muffled gong. After a quick splash of water over our faces from a bucket, we had our breakfast of sweetened rice with milk and a cup of tea, seated at rough wooden tables. We were again instructed to remain in a close group together and not split up into little groups.

It was stifling hot and, even as we started off, we could see the dense forest ahead. We all managed to stay quite close together forming a long queue and walking at a steady pace following the army officer. Within an hour or two, we were surrounded by trees that seemed to get taller as we progressed, almost blotting out the sun. All around we heard the sounds of birds fluttering and cawing loudly. The monkeys were screeching from the trees above and the din of what we thought were crickets was sometimes deafening. We were surrounded by wildlife on all sides. We felt like intruders walking into an oppressive, unwelcome, strange world.

We were soon snaking through the tall trees up a rough unmade road, when Blanche pointed out three elephants carrying huge loads of wooden crates in a clearing just ahead, almost hidden by trees. We were later told that the crates contained our provisions and fresh water for use at the next camp.

After about two hours of walking, we came to a clearing in the forest where we were told we could stop for a short rest, the slow walkers catching up with those slightly ahead. There was a general sense of relief that we were into what we thought was the last difficult leg of our journey. Many of us were impatient to press on. We would be safely at the Indian border in seven days. We spoke of our great plans - meeting up with Eugene, then on to Aunt Agnes who would even now be preparing for our arrival in Lahore.

Soon we continued on in an orderly manner with our

little belongings, Blanche carrying the bag on her shoulder containing our money and father's papers, Richard carrying a grip, and Nath the two small cases. Helen seemed calmer, carrying her teddy bear, holding my hand, and walking along the narrow rough path just ahead of Blanche, Richard and Nath.

There were a few elderly ladies struggling with their holdalls, many mothers with young children, some of them carrying their babies on their hips and in slings on their backs.

We were tired, hot, thirsty and hungry when we arrived at our first camp in the late afternoon and caught sight of a long row of huts, built on a slight rise that had been cleared of trees. Logs and debris from the sawn trees littered the ground and Nath said he thought these huts were put up in such a hurry that they had no time to clear up the debris. He said they were unlikely to last through to the next monsoon. The huts were divided into small sections just as in the previous camp. The floors were formed from dry, dusty, well-trodden earth. There were four bunk beds inside each section, strung with coir rope; each covered with, a thick cotton blanket. Nath was not so lucky. Servants were allocated a large hut that they all had to share together. Roughly strung beds were lined up along the walls, fixed to the ceiling.

The lavatories were in separate rows of tiny huts a short distance from the sleeping quarters. We held our noses, for the sight and smell of them made us want to vomit. Each of these was about three square feet. A plank of wood was placed each side of a deep hole in the ground, filthy with excrement and covered in flies. This was where we were expected to relieve ourselves. When Helen saw the filthy gaping hole, she refused to go anywhere near it and started screaming, saying she wanted mummy, she wanted to go home. I said I would go into the bushes but Richard said that was not allowed; we had to be brave, we were to use these toilets. It was Blanche who took the first step when Richard said there was nowhere else we could go. Slowly she persuaded Helen and me to follow in after her. We were all quite sick when we came out and headed towards the wash room where the buckets of water for washing our hands were also stinking dirty and swarming with flies.

We were later brought a bucket of clean water for all-over washing: one bucketful for each family. The washing area was located round the back of each hut, just a small square having the same rough thatch walls, open to the sky, with drains dug in the earth leading off into a main drain running along the length of the row of huts. A plank of wood was placed in the mud on which we could just balance ourselves while splashing one handful of water at a time over our grimy bodies, the water running off and turning into slushy mud before it reached the drain. Helen was usually the first to have a wash-down, with Blanche helping her, then Blanche and myself. By the time it came to Richard's turn, the bucket was nearly always empty.

After we had washed and got our bearings, we saw that everyone had gathered round in a circle in a shady clearing near the huts. As the sun went down, small fires were lit to keep animals at bay and spirits high. We were shown into one of the larger huts having long wooden tables and benches where people were taking their place for their first meal. This consisted of boiled rice covered with a watery dark sauce that had a curry flavour, and a slice of corned beef, all served on a banana leaf. As much water as we wanted and a cup of hot tea without milk or sugar completed our meal. This was our main meal of the day. We were hungry and ate ravenously, but we could have no more. Food and water that had to be transported by elephants had to be rationed, we were told. Richard joked that he should have smuggled a few tins of sardines and cheese in his pockets from the case of food father had given us. With hindsight, he said he should have done it. "But let's not worry", he said. "We're here and this is just for a week. We're not likely to starve in that time, eh?"

After we had eaten, most of the older folk in the group were in good spirits. So too were we, caught up in general good humour and friendliness. There were many children in the group, but we were the only four not accompanied by a parent. When asked why we were alone, Richard replied that both our parents were on their way; they could well have left Monywa by now. They were sure to be in the group following. "If not in the next group, they are not far behind. Given more time, father would have been better prepared and have arranged the trip better. He would have organised proper transport and coolies to carry food and water. They'll catch up in no time at all," he boasted.

Blanche got chatting to a lady seated next to her, about mother's age, who had two girls, aged about eight and eleven, whose husband was still carrying on with his job as a railway inspector in Mandalay. Both girls were carrying bright red and blue tapestry 'Shan' bags over their shoulders, full of books and toys. Their circumstances were very much the same as ours in having to leave their home at short notice, their father still manning his job.

Many of the people we spoke with had shocking stories to tell. Some from Rangoon had been in their air-raid shelters and had actually seen their homes destroyed by the barrage of bombs that rained down from Japanese aircraft. Many told of looting by local Burmese people following such attacks and how law and order had broken down due to lack of policing. There were also remorseful people in our party who told of how some of their family members had died of fatal injuries received during the bombing raids, how they had hastily buried them in shallow graves, unable to give them any kind of ceremony before leaving. They told horrific stories of abandoned and wild dogs roaming the streets, and of crows and vultures swooping down on areas strewn with debris and dead bodies. We agreed that we were lucky to have escaped the bombing, unlike many of our travelling companions, and not to have witnessed such ghastly scenes.

Many of the people we spoke to, like us, were looking forward to seeing their families in India who awaited their arrival in Calcutta. Great reunions were being planned all over India when they arrived back.

As darkness fell, we all helped in gathering twigs and wood to keep the fires alight. We were a very lucky group, for a young man had brought his guitar, another a mouth organ and, before too long, they had struck up a few melodic chords. Soon we were all joining in the tuneful songs we had been hearing on the wireless these past few months: 'It's a Long Way to Tipperary', 'It's a Lovely Day Tomorrow', and many more. We were caught up in happy merriment that first evening. The bond of friendship that formed between us was truly extraordinary. Even Helen and I forgot mother for a few minutes as we joined in the singing and clapped our hands in time with the music in convivial camaraderie.

Day Two

The second day of the trek started early. We were woken from a deep sleep to the loud clanging of gongs. Nath was already at the entrance of our hut, shouting at us to get up and get something to eat before it was all cleared away. He had eaten already and had filled flasks and bottles with drinking water. After we had breakfasted on chappaties with lentil soup and a cup of tea, we all gathered together in the clearing outside for the head count. Having got to know some our fellow travellers the previous evening, we were in good spirits.

Richard had struck up a friendship with a tall, well-built and friendly man in his early thirties who was travelling alone; his name was Simon. He was carrying a big gun in a heavy leather case. He realised that we four were making the journey on our own without an adult except for Nath. Seeing that we were struggling with Helen who had to be carried most of the time on Richard's back through streams and steep rocky paths, he asked if he could be of help. Richard was only too happy to have a companion and someone to lend a hand. Richard, in turn, offered to carry Simon's gun. Simon said it was the only thing he had had time to grab before leaving his home in Rangoon just hours before the Japanese entered the city. There were times during the journey when Richard found the gun heavier to carry than Helen, but they happily enjoyed each other's company and the gun was passed from one to the other, as was Helen, for the rest of the journey.

As we trudged along, young and old, rich and poor, we noticed that many elderly folk and the women carrying babies and young children were finding it very difficult to manage the rough, narrow steep paths. The streams were particularly hazardous to walk through and there were a few who slipped and had to be helped along by the coolies who accompanied us. There were a few able-bodied men among us who were always willing to give a helping hand.

We picked our way slowly through narrow paths with massive jagged rocks on either side. In places, we had to scramble up steep hills on all fours and slowly down small ravines. Some of the paths wound round thickets of thorn, bamboo, massive trees and tall elephant grass, and we stumbled over the roots of trees, overgrown and hidden by thick creepers.

We stopped when one or other of our group stumbled and fell, often needing bruised knees and wrists to be attended to and causing us to fall behind the main party. One old lady, weary and drained of colour, stopped and leaned against a huge rock. Tired and worn out, she pleaded between short breaths, "I'll have to stop here. Please don't wait. Please go on. I can't keep up and I don't want to hold you up. Don't wait for me. Please leave me here. You go on." People gathered round, trying to reassure and help her. "You can rest at the next camp," they were saying. "It's not far to go now, just a few hundred yards. We can't leave you here." After some gentle persuasion, she was able to rejoin the group, having to be carried some of the way because of a painful blister. She reached camp eventually in a pitiable state. When we started out the following morning, we looked out for her but she was nowhere to be seen. Richard told us she would probably follow with the next group after a few days' rest.

We took short breaks in high clearings and were encouraged to admire the view of the valley below that we had traversed two or more hours before. From this height, the stream or river bed was a memorable sight, zig-zagging between close mountain ranges covered in thick jungle.

Day Three

On the third day, we walked with Mrs Ellen Barker and her three children. Heather and Denise were about twelve and thirteen, and David about eight. She told us that her husband, like our father, was still at his post in Mandalay. They too had decided to leave without her husband for the safety of the children. We soon made friends with the two girls and told them of our plans for meeting up with our families in India at the end of our journey. The walk seemed somewhat easier now that we had friends to keep us company.

Now we were quite high in the mountains and, because of the misty low cloud in the mornings when we woke up, we were hardly able to see more than a few yards in front of us. Sometimes it persisted for most of the day. There were no landmarks and, without a guide, you could well get lost in the thick jungle. As usual, we had been told the night before that we were to keep close together in a tight pack. The army sergeant instructed us in a most serious tone of voice to watch out particularly for muddy swamps and squelchy streams. "Watch your every step and tread very carefully. These are very slippery places. If you fall and hurt yourself you will hold up the whole group. Besides, small scratches can easily turn septic in this hot, humid climate and turn into ulcers. Be warned – proceed with caution!"

When the sun went down, it suddenly turned cold and we were glad to warm ourselves by the fires that were lit every evening. But there was no way of avoiding the vicious mosquitoes during the night as we tossed and turned in our uncomfortable beds. One morning Helen woke up with a tiny bite on her arm which she couldn't stop scratching. By the afternoon it was red and swollen, so Blanche took her to the medical officer who treated it with antiseptic cream and covered it with a plaster. Fortunately it did not develop into anything more serious, but there were a few people whose limbs were bandaged, presumably suffering from ulcers and other injuries.

Day Four

We were well into the fourth day of our trek when Mrs Barker's son, David, began to feel ill. By midday he was hot to the touch, burning with a high temperature. He was also feeling queasy and was sick a few times. Ellen struggled to hold and guide him along as he walked unsteadily, leaning hard against her. Both Richard and Simon in turn volunteered to help David, for which Ellen couldn't thank them enough. So our little party of ten were falling behind the main group as we shuffled Helen, David and the gun between us, at the same time trying to manoeuvre our way through rocks, loose stones and uneven roots that form the jungle floor.

Blanche too was having trouble with the bag she was carrying, moving it from one shoulder to the other as it seemed to get heavier each day. The coolies who had been allocated to help carry luggage and young children during the first two days were no longer with us; they had been assigned to other duties at the camps as many people were suffering from exhaustion and needed extra care.

As the day wore on, it became even more humid and sticky; we were worn out and our progress was slow. We were all weary and in need of a cool drink. Nath's clothes were dripping with sweat. Richard realised that Nath was struggling with the cases and, though he was very tired, he did not complain but stoically struggled on, sometimes carrying the cases on his head. Richard told Blanche he thought the cases were getting too much and they agreed that Nath would be better employed helping with Helen and David than carrying the cases.

At our next rest break, Richard and Blanche had a little discussion and it was decided that we abandon our cases. It was too much to expect Nath to carry them. So it was that he put them down by the path behind some thick vegetation. I cannot say if we thought someone following might rescue them and carry them to the next camp. Perhaps we were hoping so, for they contained all our worldly goods, the beautiful painting of mother and father, the silverware that had been in the family for years, other family mementoes and all our clothes.

Blanche tried to be cheerful. She said, "We're nearing the end of our journey; we're all safe and well, we have enough money to replace our clothes and buy any other bits and pieces when we reach India. No need to worry!" To Mrs. Barker's immense gratitude and relief, Nath was now free to carry David. She thanked us for helping her son but was sorry that we had sacrificed our belongings.

By the time we reached our rest camp late that afternoon, David was delirious with fever. Mrs. Barker was beside herself with worry. Immediately on arrival she took him to the medical officer, who diagnosed that he had contracted polio. He informed her that David would not be able to continue the journey; he would have to stop here and be put into isolation right away, to rest and get proper treatment.

Mrs Barker was now faced with a terrible dilemma. She was forced into making the most heart-rending decision of her life. She argued that, if the family stayed until David recovered, which might be weeks, they might run the risk of being caught up in the military conflict. She could not contemplate the thought of her girls falling into the hands of the Japanese. She had heard horrendous stories of how young girls were being put into what was known as 'comfort houses' to entertain and 'comfort' battalions of troops. She had an instinctive need to get them to safety at all costs.

She decided that night to leave David in the hands of the medical team at the camp and continue the journey with her daughters, Heather and Denise. We were now just three days away from the Indian border. She would make sure her daughters were in safe hands in India, then return for her son, she told us. She was a strong woman physically, and mentally determined. She had to do it, and she could do it, she said. There was no alternative.

Mrs Barker was understandably very upset at having to leave David; it was an enormous personal sacrifice, but the following morning she joined us with Heather and Denise as we gathered together to continue on our way.

Much later when we were reunited with our own

family, Richard tried to discover whether Mrs Barker had returned to fetch David, and whether he had recovered from his illness. But there was no way we could get in touch with the Barker family, for we were to go our separate ways, travelling hundreds of miles to our different destinations.

Day Five

By the fifth day, we were all walking in a kind of daze, automatically following instructions to gather around our leader. It was quite noticeable that our numbers were dwindling as the days went by. Many of the friends we had made the day before were absent this morning. Richard said they were taking longer rests at camp. They would follow, he said, with the next group.

Although it was early, the temperature was already rising and as we set off many of us were dragging our sore feet. A few were limping but had found stout sticks of bamboo for support. Prickly heat caused us constant discomfort with itching and scratching.

As we progressed slowly, the jungle seemed to become ever more impenetrable; the paths became narrower with hairpin bends making their way up steep banks, then down deep ravines. From a high point you could just see the swirling water of the river below. The track led us through solid walls of green jungle, tangled and sometimes impassable, with dead bamboo strewn across which we had to get around. The slippery roots of trees and debris underfoot caused many of us to slip in the dirt. In places, we would have to stop every few yards, when a Gurkha soldier would walk back to check on people who could not keep up with the main party, helping those needing assistance. Day after day we trekked, reaching the campsite in the late afternoon, always tired, always dirty and always hungry.

We spent our evenings and nights in the same type of temporary hut, built sometimes on a slight rise, sometimes in a dugout section. The walls were of thatched bamboo, the floors of mud, with the covered area containing bunk beds only, in the same layout as the first. The same horrid, dirty, smelly latrines. No more than a bucket of water per family for washing only. Nor did the food vary much except that there was no more bully beef, just a thin lentil soup and rice or chappaties for our main evening meal and a cup of hot tea, no sugar. Each evening after sundown, the forest seemed to come alive with the sound of monkeys screeching in the trees and toads croaking in pools of water. The noise continued well into the night but we were too tired to be kept awake.

Every morning after a breakfast of boiled rice and a cup of tea, we continued our journey through the deepening forest – the trees seeming to get taller and denser as we continued further into the jungle. The heat and humidity was becoming unbearable during the day, while the nights got colder as we climbed further up into the mountains. We were surrounded by dense forests, dark and frightening at times, and passed through deep gorges running through steep cliffs. We had to watch every step we took. A number of us were injured in the foot by spiny shards of bamboo, sharp as needles and as hard as nails, about five inches long. Several members of the group were finding it hard to keep up with the main party and began to lag behind.

We had not changed our clothes since we abandoned our cases two days ago and tried to rinse off the dirt from what we were wearing in any water that may have been left over. Richard laughingly said, "Who's the smelliest today?" or "Who's the grubbiest today?" We would all shout: "I am!" Prickly heat caused us to itch all over. In spite of being reminded countless times that a slight bruise could become an open sore which could then develop into an ulcer, we could not stop scratching. Our shoes were in need of repair and Richard's blistered heels were causing him to limp slightly. We were all tired at the start the day and exhausted by the end of it.

Blanche was finding the bag of money and papers getting heavier by the day. We had left home wearing flimsy sandals, and today the strap of one of my sandals broke so I shuffled along in an attempt to keep it on. When we arrived at camp that afternoon, Richard found a piece of string and tied the sandal to my foot. I still struggled to keep it on, delaying our little group by constantly having to stop to re-tie the string, falling well behind the main column of walkers.

By the end of the day a number us were feeling the strain. Some had thorns in our feet which had to be cut out with razor-sharp hunting knifes carried by the Gurkha soldiers, some were suffering with diarrhoea and vomiting, some had been bitten by myriads of tiny creatures that roam the jungle floor. Nearly all were suffering from cuts, bruises and mosquito bites. But worst of all were the tiny sandflies that were a constant irritation round our eyes and mouths, from which there was no escape.

That evening there was very little drinking water at the camp. Richard went to ask if there might be a stream nearby where he could collect some fresh water to have a proper wash. He was told that if he followed the little path to the west of the camp, there was a small stream where the water was known to be clean.

After a chat with Simon, they both decided to go in search of some much needed water. So they set off, each with a bucket. Blanche reminded Richard that they would have to be back before five, curfew time. The authorities were continually reminding us of this. But now Richard and Simon had been gone for two hours. Blanche was getting more and more agitated, not knowing whether to report them lost or give them another five minutes before she raised the alarm. She tried not to convey her fear to Helen or me. She broke out in a cold sweat and went to our hut and lay on the bed, unable even to think. It would soon be dark but she dared not tell anyone of her fears, not even Mrs Barker. She just waited and prayed that Richard and Simon would return before curfew. The constant warnings kept ringing in her ears: "We cannot take responsibility for people wandering off and getting lost in the jungle. You can become completely disorientated in surroundings such as these, especially in the dark. No one can be spared to look for you. Robbers and dacoits roam the jungle in gangs and are known to be ruthless and to kill for little more than the shirt on your back. You will have only yourself to blame if you take any risks and get left behind."

Then, thankfully, just minutes before the gong rang out at five-thirty for the start of curfew, both Simon and Richard appeared, each carrying a bucket of water. Blanche wept with relief as she hugged them both. It was only then that I realised what a risk they had taken. But we soon forgot our worries as we drank our fill of cool, crystal clear, refreshing water. So too did Mrs Barker, Heather and Denise. We even had a little left over to splash over our faces.

Day Six

On the sixth day, we woke up to the sound of pouring rain. It was coming down in sheets off the thatched roof and collecting in pools. The whole valley was loud with the noise of wind, rain and thrashing trees. But by the time we had finished our breakfast of chappaties and dhal, the rain had eased off and we were instructed, as usual, to gather together in the central clearing. The coolies were told to start a fire. We waited for a while wondering whether we would be permitted to continue on our way or required to take shelter in our huts.

However, the rain stopped after about an hour and the sun came through the canopy of trees. It was hot again by the time we were given the order to proceed on our way through wet and sticky mud. Every tree trunk was completely hidden by creeping vines, canes and rattan hanging in great festoons from tree to tree, loosened by the strong wind so that the entire forest seemed to be linked together. This morning, the monkeys were so noisy they sounded like a pack of puppies all howling at the same time.

We were about an hour into our journey when we came to a little stream. It was just a gentle trickle of water and most of the walkers ahead of us were able to walk close to it while still keeping their feet reasonably dry. But some of us were slow, struggling to keep up. Richard was carrying Helen first on his back, then in front. Some elderly folk with sore feet and sprained ankles were making their way slowly using sticks, and needed help with almost every step through the slippery mud. Others were determined to struggle with their lifelong possessions in bags that looked too heavy.

It was a while before we arrived at the stream crossing. Imperceptibly, the flow of water had increased by the time we reached the stepping stones and was flowing swiftly over them; further down it had swollen almost to a flood. The stones were completely covered by this time and Richard, carrying Helen on his hip, walked slowly and carefully, picking his way through the loose stones and rocks. Suddenly he slipped with Helen under him, Helen bumping her head, which started to bleed. Richard recovered quickly and, after checking what he said was a slight graze, deposited Helen on the far side and re-crossed the stream to help Blanche and me over the now fast-flowing stream. We walked slowly, carefully treading our way through and eventually making it safely across, getting soaked from the waist down. When we got across, there were leeches as big as slugs sticking to our legs, causing us to cry out more in fright than pain. We all helped each other to pull the leeches off, which was just horrible as they bled profusely. Fortunately Helen was not badly injured, but we witnessed the fall of an elderly lady who refused at first to attempt any crossing when she saw how deep the water was and how we were having to pull off leeches. She demanded to be carried by the coolies, who were already overburdened. But after a great deal of persuasion, she attempted the crossing after all. She was very unsteady on her feet and unfortunately fell heavily half way across the stream breaking her wrist, which had to be bandaged in cotton strips torn from her petticoat. She was in a great deal of pain as she tried to stifle her moans. Everyone stopped to help her along to the next camp, where her wrist was properly treated and bandaged.

And so we continued, with the heat each passing day becoming more and more unbearable. Blanche said jokingly that she couldn't understand how her bag was getting heavier, but otherwise never complained. Many of us, including me, were suffering with diarrhoea. But remembering David, I told no one of my terrible stomach ache; I was terrified that I might be left behind if they found I was suffering from some dreadful infectious disease.

At the end of each day, we were always hungry and exhausted. Richard had to carry Helen most of the time now as her sandal straps had broken too, and walking on the rough, loose rubble caused her feet to be sore and painful. Blanche struggled on stoically, finding her bag heavier with each step. The strap of the bag had made red weals on her shoulders. Nath was also struggling. He had a thorn in his toe, which had to be removed. We all needed some sort of treatment on arrival at the next camp.

The only things we carried now were the bag of toiletries and a box camera. It was fortunate that father had loaded this with film, so we were able to take a few photographs on the way. Richard would line us up and say, "Come on Helen. It's not so bad, give us a smile. Mum and dad will be able to see these soon. They'll be so proud of you. Let's see how brave you are. Say cheese!" And Helen would beam a smile at the thought of seeing mother again.

Day Seven

On the seventh and last day, we were all up earlier than usual, full of expectant hope. There was great excitement, a general hum of happy chatter and laughter throughout the group, expressing hopes about what they planned to do first on reaching India. We spoke smugly of our families waiting to welcome us into their home, of returning to normal life. At the end of this day, we would be in our last camp – the last hut where we would spend our last night. Today, we would be walking the final ten miles of our journey on foot.

After a downpour of rain the previous night, the

clearing at the centre where we gathered had turned into a quagmire. As we set out, we squelched through thick wet mud. Richard remarked, "Thank your lucky stars we're not having to do this during the monsoon!" Soon the sun came out. It became hot and humid and we could see the steam rising from the jungle.

We had been told that our next port of call was Sealdah, a small town on the outskirts of Imphal. Richard told us enthusiastically that we would be in Imphal that night and that our next stop would be Calcutta. Good, caring folk were waiting to receive us and perhaps tend our sore feet. By this time, we were covered in flea bites, but Blanche was positive. She said, "All we really need is nothing more than a cool bath, clean clothes and a good meal." We told each other that, at the end of this day, we would be sleeping in a proper room in a proper bed, between clean sheets, with a pillow on which to put our weary heads.

We were all in great spirits, forgetting our smelly, hot, perspiring, bodies, our sore feet, the Japanese and all the difficulties of our recent journey. Richard and Blanche were already planning the train journey to our aunt in Lahore and impatient to relate to mother and father the adventures of our trip.

It was about noon when we reached a clearing in the forest. Our Gurkha guides pointed out what we had been straining our eyes to see through the low mist – a row of colourful buses just visible through the trees. We had reached the border. A great cheer went up, a smile on every face. Mrs. Barker, Denise and Heather, Simon, Nath and the rest of us, all were ecstatic. Our leader had told us that morning that buses would be waiting to take us across the Indian border to Imphal. A train would be waiting at Imphal to take us on to Calcutta. Had we been walking for just seven days? It seemed a lifetime! Now at last, we were here! Mum and Dad would be really proud of us. We had walked seventy-two miles.

Arrival at the Indian Border

Now we all converged around a small group of British officials. They were seated at a roughly constructed table made of bamboo. Various papers and documents were scattered over it. The Gurkha guides told us to form a queue, as we would all need to give the officers our full details. Our names, where we had joined the convoy, our destination and other information had to be recorded. Naturally we were excited, in spite of being tired and uncomfortably hot; all we wanted was to get a seat on the bus and be away, back to civilisation. It was a long, slow process. Some people sat on the newly hewn logs, waiting their turn. Helen was hot and cranky and moaning with discomfort. Her feet were sore and she had a scratch on her arm, which was red and swollen. We waited patiently in line until, at last, it was our turn. Richard was now giving our names to a British Army officer.

The officer asked in a short, clipped tone, "Who are you with? Where is your parent? Mother, father?"

Richard answered, "We're on our own, sir, myself

and my three sisters and Nath, our servant."

"Have you an adult travelling with you? Who's in charge of you? Your guardian?" the official demanded impatiently. He had a red puffy face with a bulbous nose and bulging eyes. He was sweating profusely. He too was hot, sticky and uncomfortable. He had a form in front of him, and it was his job to fill in the space for the name of parent or guardian accompanying children. He couldn't get any sense out of these kids.

"No," answered Richard, "We're on our own, with our servant. Our mother could not travel with us, she was too ill. Father could not leave his post, nor could he leave my mother. It was my father who put us on the ferry at Monywa. He said we were fit and well enough to make the journey on our own. He put me in charge of my sisters. He told us that we were to make our way to Lahore where our aunt is waiting for us."

"On your own?" the officer barked. "This is not right, it is not lawful! We have no provision here for unaccompanied children. You will have to go back to your home. Where is it? Yes, Monywa. You four will all have to return to Monywa." He put his pen down on the table as if to dismiss us. His job was done.

Richard trembled, trying to control his worst fears. For a moment he was lost for words. Blanche broke down in tears as she tried to comfort Helen. I sensed the tension and tried to hide behind Blanche, wishing father was here now. This nasty man looked stern and horrible with his loud gruff voice and bulging eyes – a thoroughly bumptious bully.

Richard said, "I can't expect my sisters to make the journey back to Monywa, sir. You can see the state they're in. They're tired. They have sore feet. Two of my sisters have lost their shoes. We had to abandon our suitcase of clothes. We have no clothes, only what we're wearing now. It's taken us over two weeks to get here, sir. I cannot take them back now." Richard brushed away a tear, trying hard to be brave and stand up to this bloated bully.

"I have no authority to allow you to cross the border," said the officer contemptuously.

Richard pleaded, "Please, sir, I cannot take my sisters back. If we are not allowed to go on, we will have to stop here. They cannot walk any further. Nor can I."

The officer looked us up and down. He could see that Richard was telling the truth. Helen's face was blotchy and dirty with crying. Helen and I were wearing thin cotton dresses that were stained with grime and dirt. We were terrified that we might have to walk back to Monywa.

"Have you got any documents, papers of any kind?" he asked.

Richard helped Blanche open up the bag she was carrying and took out some of father's papers to prove we were who we claimed, and that it was father who had made the decision for us to make the journey in the first place. The officer scanned the papers. They were to do with father's pension and insurance. They also confirmed that he was employed in a government post in the Post & Telegraphs Department. Blanche also took out the medals that father had been awarded in the First World War. The officer then stopped to consult his colleagues round the table. They all studied the papers in turn, then studied us four standing there, all looking skinny, dirty, tense and scared.

Eventually, after what seemed like an eternity, the bumptious officer said, "Even though this is most irregular, we have decided to let you through."

"Thank you, sir." said Richard.

Stretching out his arms, Richard gathered us together and wept with relief, wiping his tears in the sleeve of his dirty shirt. He said, "It's okay girls, we'll be fine."

No words can describe the relief we felt as we took our places on the bus. It was hot, it was uncomfortable, it was crowded, but what joy to know we had made it. We were safe. The worst was over. We would soon be with Aunty Agnes in a safe, normal environment and be taken care of.

We were not the only ones without shoes. Many people in the group were shoeless, their clothes in tatters. Some were quite sick with dysentery and malaria. Nearly all had sore feet. We must have looked a pretty grim and ignominious lot that day, but we were mighty pleased that we had made the journey and were safe.

We reached the end of our bus journey at Sealdah, a small town in India, a few miles from the border, and waited a short while before boarding the train. We dozed fitfully as the train chugged along slowly. It took us just a few hours to reach Calcutta. Simon and Richard figured the group had been reduced by about a third since the start of the trek.

Richard said we were lucky to have made it. He said his only moment of real fear was when the British officer told him we would have to return to Monywa. Nath, always a close protective presence wherever we were, was also relieved.

Arrival in Calcutta, 1942

I have only a hazy memory of what happened during the next few weeks, but what stands out in my mind is being provided with new clothes and shoes by kindly ladies of the British Red Cross. We were shown into a large hall where there was an array of clothes that we were told we could choose from. I chose a lovely soft silky dress printed with rows of Egyptian figures. It was loose and comfortable and had long sleeves. It hung from my shoulders so I was lost inside. And proper shoes!

I remember relaxing in a blissfully cool bath and lying in a clean, comfortable bed. I remember too hearing low, caring voices and the feel of gentle hands. I felt the glorious relief of being free from hunger and pain.

When I woke up, I was alarmed and bewildered by my new surroundings. I found myself in the antiseptic world of a hospital ward. There were nurses rushing about in their spotless blue uniforms. One was fussing over me, holding a red rubber bag of ice on my head. I asked the nurse hesitantly and fearfully why I was here. Where were my brother and sisters? Were they safe? How long had I been here? And why was I so afraid to tell them I had wet my bed? I must have passed out again, for I could hear a soothing voice, just beyond my consciousness, saying that all my family were well and that they would be visiting me the following day.

And before many hours had passed, or so it seemed, there were Blanche and Helen at my bedside. They said I had passed out in the bath; I was burning with fever and had been violently sick between bouts of shivering. They had wrapped me in towels and blankets and brought me to the hospital, none of which I could remember. Blanche said the doctor had told her that these symptoms were consistent with malaria and that I could be confined to bed for weeks.

I asked Blanche why Richard had not come with them. She reluctantly told me that he was in the men's ward of the same hospital, suffering from severe dysentery.

During this time, countless numbers of refugees were streaming into Calcutta from Burma at an extraordinary rate. Many had made the same journey as us and been struck down similarly by illness soon after arriving in Calcutta. The hospital was being overwhelmed with sick and injured people, many having to be treated in corridors. Patients like Richard and I were being dealt with as quickly as possible to make room for the next intake of sick refugees waiting to be admitted.

Richard and I were both discharged from hospital after two weeks or so, but I was not wholly cured of my illness and experienced recurring attacks of malaria for several years after this episode. Each group of new arrivals told of conditions getting progressively worse along the route. They said food and water supplies were running low, that medical staff were being stretched to the limit and that medical teams were critically short of medicines.

Eugene in Delhi, March, 1942

When initially Eugene had received father's telegram to say we would be arriving, he was stationed at Deolali, near Bombay, some distance away from Calcutta. Father had given him the approximate date of our arrival and as much detailed information as possible as to where we would be, asking him to meet us in Delhi where we were expected to spend a few hours before catching our connecting train for the onward journey to Lahore. So Eugene lost no time in taking the leave he was entitled to and proceeding to Delhi.

When he arrived in Delhi, he was faced with some chaotic conditions. There appeared to be no timetable for the arrival and departure of trains; you were not sure which platform your train would be arriving at or whether your connecting train would be arriving at all. Nobody knew. There was disorder and confusion everywhere. Also, numerous refugees were milling about with nowhere to go. The waiting rooms were full. On the streets near the railway station, people were searching for relations or friends, holding tiny photographs, asking new arrivals if they had seen this person or that.

When Eugene arrived at Delhi station on the day we were expected according to father's itinerary, he was totally taken aback to see Aunty May, mother's sister, and her husband Tom among the crowds of people waiting on the platform. They had also received a telegram from father telling them the expected date of our arrival, asking them to meet us in Delhi in case Eugene could not. They had travelled all the way from their home in Samasata.

But as things turned out, we did not arrive on the appointed day. Eugene, Aunty May and Uncle Tom waited on the platform until dark that first day, and the day after. Trains were coming in and going out and, after searching the platforms, they became more and more concerned, wondering where we were – obviously not on any train which they had seen. They were not to know we were still in Calcutta. They scrutinised the numerous lists, posted at most railway stations and outside various government offices, of newly arrived refugees from Burma and those expected, but our names did not appear on any of these. Communication of any kind was, by this time, practically non-existent.

There was no way they could get in touch with us. Nor was there any way we could contact them to let them know that we had been taken ill and detained in hospital. After three days, Aunty May and Uncle Tom, frustrated and distraught at letting us down, felt they had no alternative but to give up the hunt and return home, leaving Eugene to continue the search on his own.

Eugene continued doggedly to try to uncover some

clue as to where we were, queuing with numerous others, making enquiries at various offices. He read the newspapers for any scrap of news that might point to our whereabouts but could find not a trace. After he had spent nearly two weeks without the faintest clue, he decided to go on to Lahore. He thought we might have slipped through Delhi unnoticed and gone straight to Aunt Agnes.

When he arrived in Lahore, he resumed his search, again looking up lists of arriving refugees, but everywhere he drew a blank. By this time, he was getting extremely worried, for father had not given him Aunt Agnes's address. He contacted many of the friends we had known in the Post & Telegraphs Department in Lahore, and begged them to look out for us and convey any information they might pick up from returning refugees.

He decided then to visit his old friend and colleague of his apprentice days, Alan Colquhoun, who was now based in Chaklala, Eugene's old training camp. Alan's mother and three sisters had been living and working in Rangoon for a number of years and had recently returned to India having left well before the evacuation process started. They had travelled by sea, direct from Rangoon to Calcutta and were back in Chaklala, living with Alan. When Eugene told his friend of our plight, Alan also became concerned for our safety and together they continued the search for news of our whereabouts. With the passing of time, Eugene was worried too that his leave was fast running out.

Leaving Calcutta 1942

As soon as Richard and I had recovered our strength after our spell in hospital, we were permitted to convalesce for a few days at the Loretta Convent, part of which had been converted into a temporary respite centre for refugees. We slept on mattresses laid out in rows on the floor. The kindly nuns worked tirelessly under difficult conditions as they tried to tend the sick, arriving every day with their varying needs, as well as providing good basic meals.

Blanche changed the coins she had left in her bag into notes; her sore shoulders were now almost healed. Helen was surprisingly healthy and cheerful. In this short period, she had started gaining weight and her feet had healed. But we were missing mother and father very much and could not help wondering why they had not yet arrived.

Now that we had recovered sufficiently to continue on our way, the Mother Superior, Sister Grace, told Richard and Blanche that we would have to move on. Our Aunt was expecting us; we had to go on as instructed by father, so Richard went off the following day to make some enquiries at the railway station about trains and costs. At the train station, the stationmaster told Richard that, as war refugees, we would be allowed free travel to a specified destination, which in our case was Lahore. Richard and Blanche were delighted at the news. She was aware that our funds were running low and that we might not have enough to pay the train fare and have sufficient left for food.

Our good friend Nath, our chief support and guardian

during the past few weeks, had been limping badly as his blistered foot had not healed, and now expressed a wish to see his folk at home. He needed to return to his village near Madras for a short rest. He made a note of our address in Lahore and promised he would keep in touch. "When the Sahib and Memsahib return to Lahore," he said, "I will join the family again." He had been with us for all these years as part of our family, and we had gone through so much together – both our past joys and our recent sufferings. He was cheerful when we needed cheering, sympathetic when we needed a shoulder to cry on, always faithful and loyal. It was a sad parting. Now we could give him nothing – not even his last wage. We embraced him with warmest feelings of friendship. But as things panned out, we never heard from Nath again, for our lives were destined to take an unexpected turn. How could he get in touch? Where would we be? We ourselves were facing an uncertain future.

The time came the following morning to wish the dear nuns goodbye. Sister Grace was sad to see us leave as we were now entirely on our own, just the four of us, and we still had a long journey ahead. She said she was concerned for us, especially as we had not yet fully recovered from our journey. But there was little she could do; every day people were arriving whose needs were greater than ours. It was Sister Grace who sent for a tonga to take us to the station and paid the driver in advance from her meagre funds.

When we arrived at the ticket office, Richard had to prove we were war refugees recently arrived from Burma, so

Blanche had to display all the contents of her bag on the counter and search for the relevant papers among those father had given us. We could sense the crowd behind us getting impatient. "These kids don't know what the hell they're up to; they shouldn't be travelling on their own," we heard them complain just within earshot. However, after a short wait, the man at the counter found what he was looking for and the necessary details were copied in triplicate and authenticated by his colleague. They disappeared into the inner office for a few minutes, reappearing with a pink piece of paper which he handed over to Richard. At last it was confirmed that we were indeed entitled to free travel on the railway and given tickets to our destination, Lahore, a journey of over a thousand miles.

Above: Helen in April 1942 outside another of the temporary thatched shelters that were constructed along the refugees' route.

Above: From left to right, Helen, Blanche and Maude in April 1942 – three girls on a long trek through the jungle. This photograph was taken with the family's Brownie Box Camera, which was packed for the trip.

8

En Route to Lahore and Samasata

So began our onward journey, bound for the address given us by father, to our Aunt Agnes in Lahore.

The railway authorities had not prepared themselves for the huge influx of refugees streaming into all the main cities of India. Travelling conditions were horrendous, with crowds of people propelling and thrusting themselves forward in their effort to get through the doors of carriages. When a train pulled up at the station, it was already overflowing with passengers clinging to the handles of doors and squeezing on to the running boards. In order to secure a seat, you had to push your way through a throng of people to get to a carriage even before it came to a standstill.

We had to wait for hours in the scorching heat to board the right train and, when we managed to squeeze into the doorway of a carriage, we had to jostle through sweaty bodies, trying to follow Richard who held on to Helen's hand, pulling her behind him. Blanche and I struggled to keep up with them. At last he was able to find some vacant seats. By some kind of persistent doggedness and willpower, he managed to find a way to overcome every obstacle we encountered along the way.

The heat, as we sat in the carriage waiting for the train to start, was stifling, and the stale sweaty odour of its packed human cargo was overwhelming. Richard reminded us, jokingly, of our outward journey with mother and father and the refreshing blocks of ice father had organised to cool the carriage. It seemed a world away from what we were experiencing now. We spoke often of mother and hoped she would not have to endure these conditions. We were certain father would use his authority to make theirs a more comfortable journey.

I have only a hazy recollection of the long journey from Calcutta to Delhi. The slow rhythm of the train seemed to send me into a trance. I can just dimly remember that it was not possible for us to buy food or water on the train. I remember that, immediately the train stopped at a station, Richard would dash off in his effort to get food and water. Hawkers were shouting their wares and carrying what looked like delicious spicy morsels of food in flat baskets on their heads, but we could not afford to buy any.

On a number of occasions when the train came to a halt, he would run off immediately, disappearing from view among the crowds for a few minutes, though it seemed an eternity and left us terrified for his safety. I was only dimly aware that he was gone. The thought that he might not make it back before the train pulled away was so frightening that I may have passed out several times. Please God: let him make it back. And by a miracle he did appear, jumping back on to the train when it was already in motion, clutching a bag of food and a bottle of lemonade or water. Blanche was going through a frightening time during the journey also, digging her nails into her forearms tightly, gazing out of the window and almost holding her breath until he returned. She kept her dark fears to herself, praying – like me – and wondering: "Will he make it back in time? Will he be caught for stealing, be flogged, or worse?"

Arrival at Lahore

When we reached Lahore, we wasted no time in making our way to Aunt Agnes's home, so keen were we to be safe in the hands of family. It seemed a very long walk to the address given us by father, before we came to a block of apartments. We did not know what to expect but the address turned out to be a small flat on the third floor. I can remember clearly going up a rickety staircase and Richard urging us on, "Come on now, not far to go. We'll soon be there. Aunt Agnes will give us a good feed and we'll have a cool shower and soon be sleeping in clean, comfortable beds. She'll wash our hair and help us get our sweaty, itchy backs cleaned properly." For by now we were teeming with lice; they were in our clothes, in our hair. I thought: "In a week's time, mother and father will be here and, like a bad dream, all this will be forgotten."

We arrived at the little door. Richard knocked. After a short while it was opened by a middle-aged woman. We could not remember our Aunt, but the lady looked as if she might have been father's sister: she was tall, dark, with greying hair and of slim build. She looked us up and down. We had never seen our paternal aunt before, as father had never got on well with his sister after a silly misunderstanding years and years ago, and to our knowledge their long-standing quarrel had never been resolved. We had no idea what to expect.

Richard said, "Oh, good afternoon madam. I am Richard, these are my sisters. Are you our aunt, Agnes Evans?" "No, I'm sorry", came the reply, "Mrs Evans did live here, but she passed away a month ago."

"Do you know where her sister Alice is?" "No", the lady said. "When I arrived, I saw no one except the landlord. I took over this apartment only two weeks ago. I did not know either of the ladies you mention. I don't know where Miss Alice went when she left here."

We just stood there for a moment, dazed, speechless. We must have looked a pitiful sight. I felt sure she would have taken us in for she looked on us sympathetically, but perhaps she had enough troubles of her own. Perhaps she thought she dared not take the risk of being saddled with four strange, mucky kids.

Richard was in full control of himself. He said, "Sorry to trouble you, ma'am."

He led us back down the rickety staircase. We were devastated; we were frightened, hungry and exhausted. We did not know where to go next. I still suffered with bouts of high fever interspersed with cold shivers, the classic symptoms of malaria. Blanche also had been unwell; she too had passed out through exhaustion and worry several times on the train journey. There was nowhere else Richard could take us to but back to Lahore railway station.

We trudged laboriously back. It seemed a very long way. When we reached the station, Richard, with his usual tenacity, found us a bench on the crowded platform and laid me down, covering me with a blanket, for in spite of the heat, I was shivering with cold and the fever was back. Blanche and Helen sat next to me while he went off in search of food.

He seemed to be gone a long time. It took him all his time and newly acquired resourcefulness and cunning to support us here. He had become a master of shrewd craftiness.

In the days that followed, he would sometimes bring us tasty morsels of scrumptious sweets, samosas, a mango or two, an apple, a bottle of lemonade. We knew he had not paid for them, for the bag that Blanche still carried over her shoulder contained neither notes nor coins – just official papers.

Not only was he was jostling in and out of crowds around food stalls on the station platform, Richard was also trying to locate Eugene or any of the Post & Telegraph friends whom father had known before his transfer to Rawalpindi ten or more years ago.

Richard would go off in his search covering miles on foot in an effort to locate places he vaguely remembered as a young child. He remembered the cantonment area where families of the Post & Telegraph lived. He told himself if he could find just one family who knew our parents in the old days and were still living here, we would be safe. He walked up one street, then another. They all looked the same.

Finally, he arrived in an area where the houses and street names looked familiar. Yes, he remembered Ferozepore Road. That's where Harold Hall lived, his friend from ten or more years ago. He remembered the other Hall boys – Leslie, Edwin and Burton. They had been the friends he had played gully-dunda with. Mr Hall had worked with father years ago. They had been our neighbours and close friends.

At last Richard reached a house that looked familiar. He knocked on the door timidly. He did not know if the family he knew were still living there or what kind of reception he would get, conscious as he was of looking like a street kid, dirty and unkempt. They might not recognise him in the clothes he was wearing. Might it be a repetition of what happened when he knocked on the door of Aunt Agnes?

This time he need not have worried. It was Mrs Hall who answered the door. After Richard's introduction, she immediately, in spite of his appearance, recognised him as being the most mischievous but likeable boy of the Manuel family. She felt no qualms about inviting him in and quickly grasped the situation after his initial explanation of our present plight. She called out to the family and they all welcomed him with great excitement, for after all these years they remembered him well. He explained how we had spent all the money father had given us, that we were living on a bench in a crowded waiting room. He told them of Aunt Agnes's sudden death and that we did not know how to get in touch with Eugene, whom we were hoping to meet up with. They asked anxiously about our parents, but Richard could only tell them that he had no news.

The Hall family was most sympathetic and opened their hearts and their home to us. We had spent ten days in the station waiting room.

In Safe Hands

Joy of joys. Refreshingly cool showers. Lathers of sweet-smelling sandalwood soap, toothbrushes, toothpaste. Squeaky-clean hair. A table laden with delicious food. Special delicacies prepared for our ailing stomachs. Clean, comfortable beds on which to rest our weary limbs. Fresh clothes. Eileen, about the same age as Blanche, shared her clothes and shoes and the boys invited Richard to take whatever he wanted from their wardrobe. A few clothes had to be bought for Helen and me as there was nothing that would fit us. The warmth of this caring and compassionate family was overwhelming. We luxuriated in their kindness and generosity.

During the time we were with the Halls, we were still trying to get in touch with Eugene. We had no idea where he was. And we spoke often of mother. Where was she? Where was father?

Many of the schools within the Post & Telegraphs community living in cantonment areas such as this had devised an ingenious method of locating families returning from Burma. When a new family arrived in the district, the children would give what information they could about them to their teachers. Lists of their names were then posted on the school premises so that information flowed in both directions, between school children and teachers, and back into homes and parents. In this way, news of families was passed round quite efficiently among the close-knit community. A number of displaced families who had lost touch with relatives and friends were traced in this way. So too were we.

The Hall children informed their teachers and fellow-pupils at school that the Manuel family had arrived and were lodging with them. It was by sheer good fortune that my cousin Vera Evans, daughter of Aunt Agnes, was at that time teaching in a school at the other end of the city, and within a day or two the news reached her. By this time, Eugene had heard of the death of Aunt Agnes and been in contact with Vera to inform her that we were expected back from Burma, letting her know where he could be contacted should she get news of us.

We were delighted to see Vera that very day. She told us that she had written immediately to Eugene, who was still on leave and staying with his friend Alan Colquhoun in Chaklala, to tell him that we had been found and were living with the Halls.

When Eugene heard we were safe, he was naturally

hugely relieved and wasted no time in catching the first train to Lahore. The meeting with Eugene was an emotional one. He was overjoyed to see that we were reasonably well. He thanked the Halls for their kindness and hospitality, and told us that arrangements had been made for us to go to Samasata, the home of Aunty May and Uncle Tom.

Our joy at being reunited with him was marred only by the knowledge that he still had no news of mother or father.

Safe in Samasata

Eugene accompanied us on the train from Lahore to Samasata, a small village located between Lahore and Karachi on the edge of the Sind Desert, where he had arranged for us to stay with Aunty May, mother's sister, and her husband, Uncle Tom. They did not have children of their own and May busied herself in preparation for all four bedraggled young people coming into her home. She said we could stay with her until mother and father returned from Burma, or as long as it was necessary. She took us in without hesitation, welcoming us wholeheartedly into her home.

Eugene was naturally greatly relieved that he had at last delivered us safely into the hands of an aunt and uncle. Now it was time for him to return to camp. He had by this time overstayed his leave by nearly two weeks. He left Aunty May's house at 2 a.m., giving each of us a kiss as we slept. He took with him all the papers Blanche had carried from Burma relating to father's service with the Post & Telegraphs Department, and his Provident Fund insurance account. He also took father's war medals, the only mementoes that had been saved from all our worldly possessions.

However, when on reaching his camp at Deolali he reported to his commanding officer, he was severely reprimanded and charged with being absent without leave. He was also informed that this would be entered in his service record and deducted from his total period of service, which would in turn affect his pension. His pay would also be reduced by this charge and forfeited proportionately.

He had covered hundreds of miles travelling around India at his own expense; had faced untold hardship and worry searching for us; now, on his return, he was being penalised for his efforts. Such is the injustice of life. Soon after this, he was found to be suffering with malaria and was told to report to the medical officer. Months of anxiety had taken their toll.

Eugene Returns to Samasata

Two months were to pass before Eugene was able to make a short trip to Samasata to check up on us after his convalescence. He was concerned that I was still weak and sickly. Helen too, although she had recovered quite well physically, could not settle in her new home and continually burst into tears for no apparent reason. She kept questioning why mother was not with us; she missed her greatly and often cried herself to sleep.

Blanche Joins the WAC(I)

Blanche, who during the last few months had shared with Richard the responsibility of bringing the family to safety, had now regained her strength and felt confident enough to think about her future. She was ready to earn her own living. Now, after some discussion with Eugene and Aunty May as to what she should do, it was decided that she join the Women's Auxiliary Corps (India). So it was that Eugene accompanied her to the nearest recruiting centre in Bahawalpur, a few miles from Samasata, for her interview where she was accepted and was enlisted in the WAC(I) as telephone operator. She was sent to Quetta for her initial training, after which she was posted to Rawalpindi.

Blanche enjoyed her independence, being posted to various places in the Punjab during those frenetic war years. There was a lot happening during that time and she met people of many different nationalities in the course of her work, including American and Australian servicemen.

Richard Joins REME

Richard had travelled with us to Samasata and, after several weeks of rest and good food, recovered his strength quite soon, confident now and not altogether guileless. He was keen to be independent and eager to be part of the war effort. From all corners of India, young men were being sought and encouraged to sign up to the armed forces. Eugene advised him to go to Chaklala, his old training camp, where his old friend Alan Colquhoun was living with his family.

Richard did in fact go to Chaklala as Eugene suggested and was enlisted in the Royal Army Ordnance Corps on the 5th June 1942. After a four month period of training, he was transferred to the workshop of the Royal Mechanical and Electrical Engineers in Kirkee, near Poona. He enjoyed and flourished in army life, later serving in the Middle East.

Left: A formal photograph of Richard taken on 28th May 1946

9

Eric and Walter Journey to India

Eric in Rangoon, January 1942

At this point in my story, I will have to roll back the years to January 1932 when Eric was still in Rangoon just weeks before the Japanese overran the city. They had continued to advance by air, sea and land across Burma. Their pilots carried out their attacks with grave efficiency. They would fly in low overhead, select and quickly obliterate defenceless towns and villages with complete disregard for any code of international warfare. They were carried on a wave of wanton destruction. Houses built of timber erupted in flames and collapsed into so much debris. Many hundreds of lives were lost as people tried to escape by the sea route, for a number of ships leaving Rangoon were destroyed by Japanese planes during the later stage of the evacuation.

It was by sheer good fortune that Eric was one of the few men mustered by the British authorities from the civil service and telegraph department for evacuation by sea from Rangoon to India in early January 1942, before the Japanese took control of the port. There was a strict policy in force for each passenger boarding these ships to be registered: details of names and occupation had to be given and recorded by army officers. So it was by an extraordinary coincidence that, a few weeks later, one of these officers happened to meet father in a lodge north-west of Monywa where they were both spending the night. Father was on maintenance duty and the army officer on his way back to join his battalion in Burma via the north-west route. He remembered Eric by name and was able to give father the news that Eric had made the journey safely to Calcutta. Father then conveyed the news to Eugene by telegram.

Walter in Lashio, Burma, 1942

The Japanese Air Force had now started sending out endless waves of dive-bombers towards Lashio, in the north-east where Walter was employed in the Post & Telegraphs Department, causing the death of hundreds of innocent civilians. Thousands more were seriously wounded, but not every bomb exploded. Often after a raid, some unexploded bombs were discovered and, in the right hands, made safe.

After one such raid, Walter happened to find one of these by the roadside, glinting in the sun. It was a beautiful object, smooth and shiny, and he could not resist carrying it back to his lodgings. He proudly showed it to his friends, one of whom was Ron, a nursing orderly in the Royal Army Medical Corps. He placed it carefully on a shelf above his bed but, when Walter returned from work the following day, he discovered that the bomb was missing. He had no idea who might have taken it. He realised he had to find it as it was live and dangerous. He made numerous enquiries amongst his friends and warned many not to tamper with it if they found it.

A few days later while Walter was lying on his bed listening to his gramophone, he heard a huge explosion in the compound, not far from his lodgings. He dashed towards the scene of the blast and discovered that a room had been completely demolished, leaving a shambles of broken glass and splintered wood. He was horrified to discover Ron lying on the floor, his face and hands bleeding, the bone in his left hand exposed. Walter tied a tourniquet round his arm while a few neighbours helped children out of the smoke-filled room. Thankfully, they had suffered only slight burns and were treated for shock, but were not seriously injured.

Ron admitted that he had taken the bomb but did not realise it was live and that it could explode if it was tampered with. He said he was fascinated by the fine craftsmanship of the gleaming piece and wanted to investigate its inner workings, and had unscrewed the bottom plate. He said he noticed the small fan, which he presumed was designed to guide the bomb to its target. He lifted it towards the oil lamp hanging from the ceiling and tried to undo the mechanism. Unfortunately, Ron said, it slipped from his grasp and crashed down on the table. This set off the detonator and it exploded. "By gum," Ron exclaimed, "it was a bit of a shock!"

The following day, the military authorities began an inquiry into this incident, but it had to be postponed because of the speed of the advancing Japanese army. When Ron reached Calcutta many months later, he tried to trace Walter whom he blamed for the resulting amputation of his hand, but after a brief investigation it was decided that Ron himself was to blame for the loss of his limb, and not Walter.

Walter Leaves Lashio

Airlifts were now being arranged by the government for people of non-Burmese origin to evacuate the townships in this area, and Myitkyina, an air base located north of Lashio, continued to operate until it could no longer be defended.

Walter continued his job as a test clerk in Lashio under difficult and disruptive conditions, being under constant air attacks. When the official order finally came for him and his colleagues to evacuate the Post & Telegraphs office they were ordered to destroy all government-owned equipment and any personal belongings they could not take with them.

They were instructed to leave immediately, taking with them only what they could carry. Walter and his colleagues organised themselves as best they could for what they knew would be a tough journey ahead. It was by sheer good fortune that Walter had visited the defence storeroom a few days earlier, where he had been supplied with a good strong pair of RAC boots and a kukri knife.

Walter's was a small party consisting of the few remaining staff of the Post & Telegraphs Department in Lashio. They left hurriedly, having no time to search for maps or compasses. Walter had just enough time to pack a small bag of clothes and a few tins of canned meat and, as it had started to rain, grabbed a blanket to cover his shoulders. He was the only one in his party to have a bicycle and thought he might be able to ride it part of the way and, as it had been a present from father, he was reluctant to part with it. All employees were informed that they were responsible for their own safety. They were given a short briefing on the best route to take, bearing in mind that Japanese forces were making steady advances in the area, and that several camps along some of the routes had been burnt down because of cholera outbreaks. They were instructed to follow the northern Hukawng route, through Ledo Road on the border with China.

For the first leg of their journey, they managed to hitch a lift on a truck and, after some persuasion and an exchange of money with the driver, Walter was able to tie his bicycle securely to the side of the truck. But he was soon to discover, when eventually the truck had to be abandoned for lack of fuel, that it was impossible to ride the bike on the rough, stony tracks. Pushing the cycle proved to be more of a hindrance, so at the next village he offered to sell it to a local Burmese man for a hundred rupees. The man proved too sharp for Walter, for, with the excuse of trying it out, he rode off and was never seen again during the short time Walter spent there.

There was much confusion during this time among the local Burmese people. Many were unable to decide whether to stay on in their villages where they had lived peaceably for decades, or to leave. Should they abandon their homes and possessions to face the hardships of a dangerous journey and possible safety, or should they face an unknown fate under Japanese occupation? If they decided to leave, they would have to make their own way to India, and what would they do when they arrived there? To them, India was a foreign country.

Law and order was breaking down throughout the country. No police authority existed to enforce it. A number of people turned to crime, knowing they were unlikely to be caught. Looting was rife. In the turmoil and chaos that followed, Walter's bag of possessions was stolen, depriving him of his change of clothes and a few tins of corned beef. He had a moment of panic that his documents had been stolen as well, but he was extremely lucky that they were safe in his jacket pocket. Without proof of identity, life might have taken a very different turn on his arrival at the Indian border. All he possessed now was his blanket and his kukri knife.

Walter and his party pressed on. The steamboats that were in operation a few days ago were now abandoned for lack of fuel. Many of the government-employed workers along the route had themselves fled; numerous small groups were making for the safety of the Indian border the best way they could. There was not much food or clean water available at the temporary camps at this late stage in the evacuation. The paths through the forest were not marked. There were no guides. They simply followed the route north. Walter and his party had to eat what they could find in the jungle – berries, bamboo shoots, plantains and soft roots. But there was sufficient rain to provide them with drinking water. The driving monsoon rains had come early, accompanied by high winds. There were heavy downpours, day and night. This added fresh hazards to their journey. Walter shivered in clothes that were soaked through and was grateful for the little protection his old blanket gave him. His group found little or no shelter at nightfall. As they continued through the jungle, it was difficult for them to find a level piece of ground to lie down that was not sodden with water. There was often no alternative but to snatch some rest by leaning against a tree, sitting on tough roots, in uncomfortable positions, rain dripping from above, mud and water beneath, trying at the same time to forget the snakes, scorpions and other creatures that roamed the forest floor.

On one occasion, Walter and his party came to a river, swollen by heavy monsoon rain, which they needed to cross. Floodwater was surging over what might have been the remains of a roughly strung bridge. On the near side, there was what appeared to be some kind of level landing stage. There was a crowd of people gathered round a flimsy raft constructed of bamboo and lashed together with rope, many protecting themselves from the downpour with colourful wax-coated parasols. People were squeezing on to this odd contraption. An old car was being loaded on to it. This was a narrow section of river; they felt certain they would be able to cross over to the other side in a few minutes.

Walter and his colleagues waited their turn and watched as the crowded raft pulled away. It had almost reached the other side when there was a sudden cloudburst. The unwieldy raft became unstable and rocked under the downpour. Suddenly a swift torrent of water caught the car broadside on, causing the raft to capsize. Men, women and children were tossed into the water, thrashing about in the swirling current, shouting for help.

The sudden volume of water and the force of the current made it impossible for anyone to attempt a rescue. Walter and his party could only look on in horror and disbelief as the tragedy unfolded. After a short while, the screaming stopped and there was complete silence. Sadly, all those on the raft perished. Soon all that could be seen floating down the turbulent river were the colourful parasols.

Walter and his group continued further up the river in silence, feeling utterly dejected and frustrated at their helplessness in not being able to save a single soul. They were later able to cross in comparative safety on a smaller, slightly more substantial raft further upstream.

As Walter's party continued through the jungle, they witnessed some harrowing scenes. They came across many dead and dying along the way, mostly old people and young children. It was obvious the journey had proved too wearisome for many, suffering as they were from exhaustion as well as lack of food and water. Some women were weeping in despair at having to leave their little children by the side of the path. Many simply lay down and died. They came across a clearing near the river where several temporary huts had been washed away. They found the bodies of a mother and child locked in each other's arms. It was evident that the whole family had stayed together and died together. In another clearing, they came across the bodies of about fifty people and, nearby, little wooden crucifixes had been placed presumably by passing Christians. Others had figures of the Virgin Mary clutched in their skeletal hands.

Walter and his colleagues attempted to bury some bodies, but the stench was so terrible and the earth so covered with overgrowth that they were forced to abandon the task. For their own safety, they had to press on. A few of them were now suffering from malaria, diarrhoea and dysentery. Some had to be left behind, too exhausted to go on, their fate in the balance. One man in the group died of pneumonia; no one could help him, for they carried no medicines. They stayed with him to the end, trying to ease his passing. They prayed together and buried him in a shallow grave before continuing on.

After twelve days, having walked nearly two hundred miles, Walter and the remainder of his party, now reduced to twelve out of a total of sixteen, arrived at Ledo Road, the northernmost border with India and China. Their party stopped in a town high in the mountains to recuperate after their gruelling walk. After a day's rest and having been provided with food and water, they were able to continue their journey into India. Here they found that conditions were no better than before they reached the border. No provision had been made for them; they were all suffering with exhaustion. Now they were very high in the mountains and the nights were extremely cold, but they pressed on until they reached Sealdah and, like us who had done this journey four or five weeks earlier, continued their journey by bus and train from Sealdah to their destination – Calcutta.

Above: A photograph of Walter, believed to have been taken in 1942 outside the Barnes' family flat in Calcutta, where he and Eric were lodging with Mrs Barnes.

10

The Family in India

Walter and Eric in Calcutta

Within days of his arrival in Calcutta, Eric was able to secure a job in the Post & Telegraphs office as a telephone operator working night shifts. He considered himself very lucky to have been offered this job at a time when there were so many people arriving from Burma, searching for work. Not being familiar with Calcutta when he first arrived, he lived in rather cramped conditions, but his fortunes were to change when he met a friend, Ronnie Barnes, whom he had known in his childhood in Lahore. Ronnie and his mother, who had also returned recently from Burma, were now living in Calcutta. This kindly lady and her son took Eric into their home and into their hearts.

Not many weeks elapsed before Walter also arrived in Calcutta. He spent a few weeks recovering from his ordeal in a home set up for refugees, where he was given fresh clothes and a few basic necessities by the British Red Cross in much the same way that we had been. As soon as he felt fit enough for work, he made his way to the Post & Telegraphs office in search of employment. Whilst registering his details, he was overjoyed to learn that Eric had already reported there and was soon able to trace his whereabouts from the register in the telegraph office. The brothers greeted each other with cries of delight and spent happy hours together exchanging stories of their experiences. Eric told of the wretched conditions he had endured during his apprenticeship days in Rangoon. Nonetheless, Walter now found him in good health, looking fit and well.

When Eric took Walter to meet Mrs. Barnes, she was equally hospitable in welcoming him into her home. The two brothers now had a home, but there was as yet no post available for Walter. However, within a few weeks, through his persistence in turning up at the Post & Telegraphs office unfailingly every morning, he was given the job of technician but, as it later turned out, this was to be a temporary post.

Father Arrives in Calcutta, May, 1942

At the time Walter and Eric were lodging with Mrs Barnes, they were hundreds of miles away from us in Samasata. Refugees arriving from Burma spoke of conditions en route becoming ever more difficult. Cholera had broken out among some groups and, because of the contamination of most streams, there was no fresh water to be had except for rainwater. Their concern for the safety and whereabouts of mother and father was mounting.

But one day, there was a knock on the door of Mrs Barnes' house. Eric had been on night duty and happened to be the only one at home at the time. He answered the door to find two of father's linesmen standing there, Banasidas and Abdullah, the same men who had accompanied father on his numerous tours up country, looking relieved that they had found Eric at last. They said they had been searching for Eric and Walter all over the city. Calcutta was, and still is, a bustling place, heaving with people and traffic, a maze of narrow little streets. It is almost impossible to track down anyone whose address is not known. They were on the point of giving up the search when, by some amazing coincidence, a cobbler sitting by the roadside, who had recently mended Eric's shoes, overheard them asking about the two brothers. The cobbler was willing and able to direct them to Eric's address. All credit is due to these loyal men for having found Eric in the labyrinth of streets and alleyways that make up Calcutta.

Banasidas and Abdullah told Eric that father had recently arrived and was now in Campbell Hospital, gravely ill. "He is in a very serious condition, sahib. He has been injured and cannot walk. We will take you to him," he said. "We must not delay, we must go now." Eric expressed the hope that father would have a good chance of recovery; he would receive proper treatment now that he was in hospital.

On their way to the hospital, the two men told Eric of their appalling journey. Eric learned that father had stayed at his post waiting for instructions right up to a few days before the Japanese were expected to reach Monywa. When eventually he did receive permission to vacate the premises, he was ordered to destroy all equipment and documents that might be of use to the enemy. He was to make arrangements for his own personal safety and those employees who wished to leave at the same time. As it happened, they were the last three to leave the Post & Telegraphs office, all the other employees having been dismissed some weeks before.

They were just days into their journey when they were caught in an air attack and a piece of flying shrapnel got embedded in father's leg. It caused him great pain and the wound bled profusely. They were able to bind his thigh with bandages but, as the days went by, the wound became infected and gangrene set in. Little could be done to treat the injury as their stock of medical supplies had not been replenished for some time and they were not carrying any. After struggling through the difficult terrain for the first few days, it became impossible for father to walk so the two men constructed a rough stretcher made from pieces of bamboo and twisted vines.

At this late stage in the evacuation, the route we had taken a few weeks before had been cut off because of extensive flooding and disease. The only route open now was the longer, more difficult one through Ledo Road on the border with China, the same route that Walter had taken a few weeks earlier. Father's group would have encountered even more horrendous scenes of the dead and dying than

Walter had a few weeks before. Diseases such as dysentery, diarrhoea, cholera and malaria were rampant.

Banasidas and Abdullah told Eric that the monsoon was well under way by the time they left Monywa. They had to trudge through thick wet mud and struggle up slippery ascents over jungle mountainsides, most of the time in clothes that were drenched in rainwater. Progress throughout was exceedingly slow, they said, so they had to take frequent stops to rest.

They were unable to carry any food and had to live off roots and berries and the occasional fish they were able to catch from the river. Who knows what else they might have had to eat along the way to stay alive on a journey that had taken them three and a half weeks. Banasidas and Abdullah explained that they had carried father for over two hundred miles – they were indeed loyal servants who endured much to get father to hospital this day.

But sadly today for Eric, who had high hopes of seeing father, and his two faithful companions, when he arrived at the hospital the doctors told him that father had passed away just an hour ago. He added that father was barely conscious when he arrived at the hospital. The medical team had done all they could to save him, but he was very weak and tired. The doctor further informed Eric that father had no papers or identification of any kind on him, and that he would need to identify the body and sign the necessary papers. Eric broke down in tears when he saw father's emaciated body. His right thigh was black and terribly swollen. He could only imagine the pain and suffering he must have endured to come to this miserable end.

Eric and Walter were later able to piece together father's last days before he left Monywa from the information they got from Banasidas and Abdullah. They told them that they were aware of the difficult dilemma father faced after we had left Monywa. He spoke of time running out, realising weeks before he was due to leave that he would have to leave and that he could not take mother with him. Physically, she was weak, hardly able to leave her bed. Mentally, she had been confused, distraught, deeply disturbed, continually calling out each of our names in turn, scarcely aware of what was happening. Father decided she was in no condition to accompany him on the journey through the jungle. She could not possibly survive the rigours of the journey. He contemplated his various options. There were not many. Should he leave her in a safe place in Burma? Where could he find such a place? Where could take her to? He agonised at having to leave her at all, not knowing what fate might befall her, what manner of suffering she may have to endure alone. All he knew was that he could not take her with him. If he stayed with her, the Japanese would kill them both as father had played a vital role in keeping lines of communication open between the armed forces and the British authorities right up to the last day.

Banasidas and Abdullah explained the trauma father had gone through. It had been a terrible choice to make – the only one open to him, of leaving mother in a safe place before his departure. He hoped that she really was in safe hands, but neither of them could tell Eric where mother had been taken.

Father died on 27th May 1942, aged 52 years.

Eric and Walter, with the help of his friend Ronnie and Mrs Barnes, arranged a funeral service for father. It was a simple burial service. He lies to this day in Tollygunj Cemetery, Calcutta.

Eric had the sad task of writing to Eugene, who at this time was in Deolali, and to Aunty May and Uncle Tom, telling them of father's tragic death, at the same time giving them the distressing news that there was still no word of mother's whereabouts.

Helen and I, and Aunty May and Uncle Tom, hugged each other with sadness on hearing the news and how he must have suffered. We felt bereft at losing him. We knew that, from now on, things would never be the same. Father was a strict parent but we thought perhaps this might have been because of the high standards he expected of us. We realised that he cared greatly for us as a family and, in spite of the punishment he had received at father's hand, Richard burst into tears and could not be consoled, for he truly loved father and knew he would be greatly missed.

As for mother, he had made the right decision in not expecting her to undertake the ordeal he had experienced himself. We felt certain he would have left her in safe hands.

Eugene Meets Eric and Walter in Calcutta

By coincidence, Eugene was sent on a short course in fire fighting to a region in Assam, near Calcutta, where allied forces were gathering in preparation for the thrust to recapture Burma. He supervised and took part in rescue work, helping in the task of putting out the numerous fires that raged throughout the city as the result of Japanese bombing. Battalions were now being assembled and trained in jungle warfare to take part in the counter-offensive against the Japanese.

Eugene had always kept in close contact with Eric and Walter through letters and telegrams, and it was during this time that he met up with them both. For a short time, all three brothers lodged with Mrs Barnes.

The brothers spent time together sharing their experiences and trying to work out where mother might be or what course of action might be taken to trace her. Circumstances at this time were such that they were often confounded at every turn by lack of information. It was proving to be a most frustrating task because of communication difficulties caused by obstructive officials in Calcutta, and confusing reports infiltrating through from Japanese-held territory.

At about the same time, Eugene was trying to obtain the necessary documentation to release funds from father's pension. He had to wade through all the bureaucratic red tape that this war-torn country could devise in an attempt to gain official custody of Helen and me. He carried on a ponderous correspondence with the Government of Burma, which had now transferred its headquarters from Rangoon to Allahabad, in the Central Provinces of India. Because he was billeted to several camps during this period, he had to make endless journeys to different courts in every new area of his many postings. He appeared before various judges who maintained that he was located too far from where Helen and I were. The children, they said, needed their guardian to be accessible and reasonably close at hand should they need to contact him at short notice. The nature of his career at present was not compatible with the guardianship of his sisters, who were residing several hundred miles away in Multan. They refused at first to grant him custody of us.

Nor could Eugene produce the proof required to satisfy officials of the whereabouts of mother, who was next-of-kin to father's estate, or even whether she was dead or alive. My brothers were also entitled to their share of father's insurance, so he was battling on their behalf also. In order that some money might be released for our immediate needs, and so that payment could be centralised to one source, he had to obtain 'no objection' letters from Walter, Eric and Richard, in order that monies due to them might be paid to himself on their behalf. At this time, Walter, Eric and Richard were enlisted in different branches of the Army, many miles apart. They could not tell where they might be posted from one week to the next. Trying to contact them to sign the necessary forms was a complex and wearisome task. However, after several weeks, when Eugene finally received the necessary authority from my brothers, they did not simply give him authority to receive their share of father's estate, they each specified independently that they wished their share to be distributed between Blanche, Helen and myself.

Eventually, after many long months and a mountain of correspondence, Eugene's perseverance was rewarded and he obtained a Guardianship Certificate from the High Court for Helen and myself. He was now able to obtain some funds from father's life insurance to make some contribution to Aunty May towards our living expenses and pay our long overdue medical and school fees. He sent Blanche a proportion of the funds he received to set her up in her new job in the WAC(I).

Samasata

Samasata's only claim to fame was that it was an important junction where trains peeled off in different directions to a number of destinations in the Punjab. A small friendly community of Anglo-Indian families lived here, nearly all employed by the North Western Railway, as was Uncle Tom.

Ever since I arrived in Samasata, I was a sickly child but, throughout the months of my illness, Aunty May treated me with the greatest affection and kindness. I could not have been looked after better had I been her very own child.

My weakened immune system could not cope with

all the viruses that were present in the air, the water, the hot earth. As soon as I recovered from one illness, I seemed to pick up another – enteric fever, chicken pox, measles, and constant attacks of malaria and tummy upsets. I became debilitated and lethargic. I just lay there, day in, day out, at times too weak to lift my head off the pillow. The doctor was a regular caller at our house, but all he could recommend besides quinine was bed rest. I was put on a strict diet of milk and milky puddings, sometimes sloppy rice cooked in milk. I was nearly always hungry and begged for something more substantial and spicy, but could not keep it down, and I continued to lose weight. Nor did I like the nickname Uncle Tom chose for me, but realised he meant it affectionately rather than a a criticism of my skinny, gaunt appearance: it was 'Succroo' (Bombay Duck) which is, as everyone knows, a long skinny dried-up fish.

Many of the English-speaking families in Samasata were Roman Catholics, but as we were not a large enough community to qualify for a local priest, Father O'Grady would visit regularly from the nearest parish town, Multan, to celebrate Mass. There was no church or community centre where services could be held, so Mass would be celebrated at the home of each Catholic family in turn where we would all congregate for the service.

On the particular Sunday I write of, Father O'Grady was expected to come to our house and give me a special blessing. Aunty May had made up my bed with her best soft cotton sheets; the whitest of white and her most treasured fancy pillowcases. They were beautifully hand-embroidered with butterflies in fields of flowers in fantastically bright colours. There I lay, pristine, under brilliant white sheets tucked up to my neck, my head making a small indentation on the highly embellished pillow, my thin hands clasped together over my stomach, ready for the priest – maybe the Last Rites. In walked Father O'Grady, a tall, well-built man with fiery red hair. He seemed to fill the whole room with his presence. A no-nonsense Irish man. He saw me lying there, clean, pure, untouched. He looked me straight in the eye and, rubbing his hands together with great panache, said in his broad Irish brogue, "My dear girl, you'd make a lovely corpse!"

I was so shocked by his words that I suddenly raised myself up on my elbows; I know not from where I got the strength. I said, "No, Father, no, I will not. I want to get well. I'm going to be well!"

I got no blessing that day. What I got was a lecture that was to be my philosophy for the rest of my days. In his forthright Irish manner he said, "Come on girl, what is this? You are not doing too badly now. You are safe, you have everything you could wish for; you have a loving family. Thank the good Lord and count your blessings that you have a kindly aunt and uncle who have taken you to their hearts; you know they love you dearly. They are concerned for you. You're causing them a great deal of worry and concern."

"Snap out of it, girl!" he ordered sharply. "It's up to you to make the effort to get well! The next time I come to Samasata, I will see you at Mass in person. I'll have no excuses!"

As soon as Father O'Grady left, I said to Aunty May, "Aunty, I'm not just going to lie here any more. I'm going to be well! And I don't want this pillow, please give me a plain one. I will not let this silly illness get the better of me. I'm going to be well, I'm not going to die."

I seemed gradually to recover my strength after this incident, maybe by force of will, but within weeks I was able to tolerate solids, gradually putting on weight and each day feeling a little stronger. Aunty made me swallow a raw egg every morning which she said was "part of my new protein-enriched diet; it would make me good and strong." She made sure I had lots of nourishing foods besides – plenty of fresh fruit, vegetables and lassie, a cool milky drink made from fresh yoghurt. I was soon joining Helen and our neighbours in outdoor games and outings to the local bazaar.

Samasata was stifling hot and dry and located in a dust bowl known as the Sind Desert. During the hottest part of the day when the sun was directly overhead, we would lie indoors on our beds under a fan made of heavy fabric, nailed to slats of wood and suspended from the ceiling. This was attached to a rope which the punkah-wallah sat and pulled to and fro in the next room, creating a slight movement of air. Sometimes he would tie the cord to his big toe while he pulled rhythmically, up, down, up, down, and in this mode would occasionally doze off himself, when Tom would wake him up suddenly with loud swearing.

The evenings were always the best part of the day.

There would nearly always be a cool, light breeze out of doors; we would sit in the garden as the sun went down, with glasses of water or lemonade, when our immediate neighbours joined us in games and convivial chat.

We dined under a bright gaslight that seemed to attract mosquitoes, moths and myriad tiny insects from all around the district, for there was no electricity in Samasata except for those lucky enough to own a generator. Occasionally, May and Tom would have friends for dinner when we were told to amuse ourselves indoors, out of their way. The little kitchen, behind which the cook had his private room, was about fifty yards from the main house.

The humidity was unbearable in the summer months. We suffered terribly from prickly heat, having to wash our sweaty bodies morning and evening. When the air became heavy and oppressive, we knew a storm was brewing, for murky clouds of dust could be seen approaching some distance away. On these occasions, we would rush inside to close the doors, windows and skylights which never seemed to fit tight enough to keep out the fine dust. It would get into every corner and crevice of the house, not to mention your ears, nostrils and hair. At night, we slept out on the veranda or in the open air, away from the building that seemed to absorb the heat during the day and disperse it at night. Sometimes in the middle of the night, we would literally have to pick up our light charpoy beds and carry them inside. These dust storms were usually followed by a heavy downpour of rain and, when it had passed over, we were thankful for the cool respite it brought, though we spent a few days mopping up, washing curtains, bedding and rugs, and generally working with the cleaning boy to get the house back to normal.

Uncle Tom

Uncle Tom was a short, dapper man. He was employed as a guard in the North Western Railway. When getting ready to go on duty, he was meticulous in his dress and appearance. His dark-blue serge suit would be brushed and cleaned, his trousers pressed to a razor-sharp crease, his shirts always a brilliant white. His brass cap badge was shone until it sparkled, as did the buttons on his jacket. His shoes also were polished to a deep shine and off he would strut, upright and erect, his belly protruding before him, followed by his faithful pie-dog, Titch. Boy, his personal servant, would be close behind, carrying his line-box containing his timetable and other papers, a red and a green flag, a railway lamp that could be switched from red to green, his sandwiches, and last but not least a small bottle of the potent local hooch. We would all wave him goodbye as he left home, and wave to him again as his train passed within yards of the house.

Multan

Twelve months were to pass before I was well enough to start school. Eugene visited us regularly throughout this time and had arranged with Aunty May and Uncle Tom for Helen and I to attend the nearest boarding school. St. Mary's Convent in Multan was the school they chose for us, where we tackled our studies with quiet determination, catching up with our age group and making up the time we had lost with me being ill. We integrated well into our new life as boarders at the Convent. In a few months, I was to become the most popular girl in school, for it was I who could run the fastest, and I who could hit the ball hardest. So it was I who was chosen to be in the rounders team!

The winter months in Multan were surprisingly cold, being on the edge of the desert: we endured very cold winters and very hot summers. Eugene realised that both Helen and I were in need of winter coats. The war was still in progress and many items of food and clothing were strictly rationed. Woollen fabric was especially difficult to obtain. Eugene was able to buy some nice soft, blue woollen material for Helen's coat, but all he could find for mine was a piece of surplus thick khaki cloth from his local army store. Off-the-peg clothes were unheard of, but the local tailors were very skilful in producing stylish garments simply by copying the styles from illustrations in magazines. When Eugene brought the coats to us at Multan just before Christmas, Helen was delighted with her lovely blue coat, though I was most disenchanted with the colour and weight of mine; but downhearted I was not. It was warm and fitted well. I wore it with pride and was instantly nicknamed 'soldier' by my classmates.

As our comparatively healthy and stable days passed

into weeks, weeks into months, and months into years, our lives were overshadowed always by a dark cloud of fear and apprehension, for we still had no news of mother. She was constantly in our thoughts and we prayed that she was well, in a safe place. Communication with Burma by post, telegram or any other means was impossible. The country was under Japanese occupation, cut off from the outside world.

Above: From left to right, Eugene, Walter, Ronnie Barnes and Eric during their short stay together in Calcutta in 1942.

Above: Walter (left) and Eric (right) in Calcutta ca. 1944 during their training with the Chindits.

11

Eric and Walter Join the Chindits

By late 1942, Japanese forces were streaming steadily towards the Indian border, meeting little resistance. Japanese guerrilla fighters won by simple infiltration, operating against conventional armies which moved and received supplies by road and rail. Small parties of Japanese forces would carry out swift and unsuspected flanking movements through the jungle, bob up from nowhere behind the British lines, destroying communications or erecting roadblocks.

Behind a barricade of teak logs, fifty or so Japanese with mortar and machine-guns would cut off the line of retreat for a whole brigade, leaving the British the choice of either waiting to be encircled by the main enemy force or charging up a narrow road head-on into Japanese fire. From the start, the Burmese fifth columnists had done their work extremely well. It was later learned that long lanes in the shape of arrows had been marked out in the fields, pointing the way to allied military defence camps. The Japanese would simply follow the direction of the arrows and obliterate the camps. There were rumours, probably

Japanese in origin, that many of the officers of the British Army and Navy, and their men, were absent from their posts because of Saturday night parties which they said made it easy for them to make surprise attacks.

It was in 1941 that politicians and military men of rank realised that the Japanese were a force to be reckoned with. Field-Marshall Viscount Wavell had all along been struggling to check the Japanese advance through Burma. He instructed Brigadier Orde Charles Wingate to organise activities against Japanese communication. The British realised they would have to change their tactics in northern Burma to fight an entirely new kind of war against the Japanese. Brigadier Wingate planned to beat them by a revolutionary system of training, transport, communication and supply. He was planning to train his men in jungle warfare under gruelling conditions – as gruelling as anything they might encounter in the campaign, until every one of them was a hardened, cunning, self-reliant jungle fighter. For transport, he reverted to pack animals – elephants, mules and bullocks. He divided his force into self-contained columns and planned to infiltrate Japanese lines, wrecking the enemy's system of communication. In the past, the Japanese had surprised the British by creeping up behind them using jungle trails. He planned to go one better and force his way, wherever possible, through virgin jungle, ambushing the Japanese as they marched along the beaten paths. His own communication lines would be safe because he would have none. All his supplies would be dropped from the air. A wireless was to provide his only contact with the outside world. With these tactics, he was preparing to operate indefinitely in enemy-occupied territory.

In February 1943, with Wavell's backing, Wingate's men were preparing to set out from Assam in the north-east corner of India. He called his band of men 'Chindits' after the Chinthy, the lion-griffin that was to symbolise for them the unique co-operation between ground and air forces. It was into this elite organisation that Eric and Walter decided to enlist after their short spell of employment with the Post & Telegraphs Department in Calcutta. It fired their imagination. They were full of enthusiasm at joining this highly trained force and swore they could and would overpower the enemy. Added to this was their determination to find mother. They felt it brought them a step nearer to finding her, or contacting someone who knew or had seen her after father had been forced to leave. Now at last they were able physically to make some contribution towards the search.

Walter and Eric were both selected to undergo their military training in Assam, India, in the mountainous region that forms part of the Himalaya range that separates India from Burma, known as 'the roof of the world'. Eric took part of his initial training in the East Coast Battalion, Vizagapatam, on the east coast of India.

The final part of Eric and Walter's training was undertaken in the sweltering heat of the monsoon season, in incessant rain and heavy mud. It was to prove an endurance test for those selected for the tough and dangerous mission now being planned. During the course of training, a number of men in their company dropped out because they were unable to endure the discipline, the arduous training, the humidity and the difficult terrain.

After his training, Walter was ordered to report to Gauhati, situated on the border between India and Burma. Having had several years' experience as a telegraphist, he was assigned to the Royal Signals Corps. After four weeks, he was transferred to Dimapur and promoted to the post of chief telegraphist. It was a job father had held before him, handling secret and sensitive material dealing with the movement of troops. He did short spells of under-cover work at Lumding, Tinsukia, Digboi and Margharita. These were small villages within twenty miles of the Indian border but located within Burma and very close to Japanese lines. The Japanese were known to be in the neighbouring area of Kohima, to the north of where Walter's party was operating. Because of this, their group was instructed always to be in a state of readiness for sudden Japanese attack. Reports from here also confirmed the appalling brutality inflicted by the Japanese; they were known to take no prisoners. It is officially recorded that they took hundreds of British and Indian troops prisoners and slaughtered them in cold blood.

Eric's knowledge of the Burmese language enabled him to become an interpreter with the rank of Lance Corporal, attached to the 17th Indian Division, South-East Asia Command of the Burma Intelligence Corps. He was stationed in the same area as Walter, but formed part of an active ground force, moving deep into enemy-occupied territory.

It was not long before Eric and his platoon found themselves in the thick of jungle warfare, slogging their way through stinking quagmires. Then deeper into virgin forests of elephant grass, the blades of which grow stiff and sharp – more like wire grass – which grow to a height of fifteen feet in places. Underfoot, the roots of trees were tangled and matted together, one mile after another. It was in these conditions that they conducted the most dangerous of military operations. Eric, along with three men, was chosen to be the leader in a tactical reconnaissance spearhead. They were in advance of the main body infiltrating Japanese-held territory. Their job was to find out from local inhabitants the location of Japanese positions and attempt to get whatever information they could of their movements.

Many of the local Kachin people were most hospitable to Eric and his comrades. Not only were they willing to help with information they had learned from neighbouring villagers concerning Japanese movements, they were also invited to share their food. They sold them chickens, rice and eggs, some fruit and often a jar of rice wine and toddy, a potent local alcoholic drink made from coconuts. They were given cheroots – special bamboo shavings loosely wrapped in green tobacco leaves. But not all the natives were friendly; in some cases they came across groups who had an ingrained hatred of the British and Indian. Eric's group had to proceed with great caution in their mission, always having to work out a route for a quick get-away before revealing themselves in case the local people proved to be hostile.

It was during one of these manoeuvres in the area of Dimapore that Eric and his comrades stumbled upon a small group of Japanese sitting round a small campfire in a clearing, preparing their evening meal. It was almost dark and they spoke in whispers.

A quick exchange of fire took place. Eric's party had taken the Japanese by surprise. A stray bullet hit Eric through his backpack, another through his ammunition pouch. A third bullet ricocheted off his boot and hit him in the shin. Blood trickled down his leg and he tried to stem the flow with his hand, still holding on to his rifle, while remaining aware of the movement of Japanese nearby. The main body of men following close behind was quickly on the scene and tackled the Japanese, some of whom escaped into the thick jungle. Five Japanese were killed outright. It was presumed that they had run out of ammunition and were waiting for supplies. Eric was the only one of his party to be injured. He was left to recover for a short while and await the medical orderly who was quickly on hand to treat him. Fortunately the injury was found to be a flesh wound and, when they reached a safer place, he was left to rest against a tree while the main party went in search of the two Japanese who had escaped in the undergrowth.

By an amazing coincidence, Walter and his group of Royal Signals were also in the area, just within the borders of Burma. His group was in the process of marching south. Walter was both delighted and shocked to see Eric, his arm and foot heavily bandaged and wearing only one boot, sitting against a tree with his rifle in his hand and his ammunition pouches lying beside him, but they were able to exchange a few brief words about this incident. Eric assured Walter that it was only a flesh wound, and that he would be able to walk quite comfortably at the rear of the column as suggested by the medic. Walter found him looking muscular and strong, broader and fitter than when he had seen him a few months before. He was in excellent spirits in spite of his injury.

Before parting, Eric mentioned that mother was always in his thoughts. He would not rest until he had found her. Walter reiterated the same hopes and feelings as they expressed their mutual concern for mother's well being.

They retold briefly some of the gruesome stories they had seen and heard of Japanese cruelty in this appalling war. When parting, Eric said resolutely, "I swear we'll get the bastards yet."

Germany Surrenders

In April 1945, America suffered a great loss when President Franklin D. Roosevelt died in his fourth term of office.

On 7th May 1945, Germany submitted an 'Unconditional Surrender' to General Eisenhower. After five and a half years of terrible war, victory in Europe had been won. This was a marvellous tonic for the Allied Forces in south-east Asia, but their war was not yet over. They had still to defeat the might of Imperial Japan.

Chindit columns operated deep behind enemy lines during 1944, and early in 1945 the 14th Army launched a successful offensive down the Arakan Coast, followed by a major advance deep into central Burma.

Eric's party formed one of many columns of Chindits. They continued against immeasurable odds to engage in jungle warfare involving great acts of courage and skill in their effort to recapture Burma. They carried out guerrilla attacks in the most gruelling conditions, during the suffocating period just before the monsoon season when the temperature sometimes reaches 120 degrees in the shade. Nerves were on edge and tempers near boiling point as the men waited for the dense storm clouds, massed oppressively overhead, to break and bring relief from the intolerable sultriness. Several men collapsed from heat exhaustion, which can quickly result in death if not properly treated. The small medical team was kept busy and under great pressure. Eric's party was involved in numerous operations to outsmart and outmanoeuvre Japanese troops, who appeared to be better trained in jungle warfare. Doubtless the men had a number of close shaves with the enemy and were involved in many bloody actions. In many instances, the Japanese were helped by Burmese who were sympathetic to their cause, providing them with food and water. But this was not always the case; there were also local people who gave the British vital information about Japanese troop movements, resulting in many an ambush.

The Japanese forces were now running short of supplies and were gradually starting to fall back towards the Irrawaddy. They were reduced to building rafts to cross the river from trees that grew along the bank. At the same time, General Stillwell's Chinese and American forces captured Myitkyina, along with its important airfield. In January 1945, the 19th Indian Division had crossed the Irrawaddy in two places north of Mandalay and succeeded in diverting Japanese troops from their real target, Meiktila. This small town was attacked by the 20th Division in February and, after a bloody battle, fell to the Allied Army on 5th March 1944.

The task of recapturing the main airfields and villages in the north-east was gradually proving successful and the British and Indian forces were moving victoriously from point to point. The operation to recapture Mandalay proved exceptionally tough but, after a fierce twelve-day battle in which losses were naturally very heavy, the town was taken on 20th March. This was the climax of the Burma Campaign, and Rangoon, the capital, was now only 400 miles south.

Disaster struck during a fierce battle at Toungoo in central Burma, halfway between Mandalay and within 160 miles of Rangoon, when Eric's battalion was involved in a separate skirmish. This was an encounter in which several companies had taken part. Major Lewton-Brain of No. 3 Platoon, Burma Intelligence Corps, attached to the 17th Indian Division, South-East Asia Command, wrote to Eugene and Aunty May with the details.

The Major wrote that a local man had informed the platoon commander of a small group of Japanese in the immediate neighbourhood; furthermore, this informant had volunteered to guide a party of men to the exact spot. He said that Eric was one of the men chosen to investigate the location of the Japanese and, as they were nearing the 'chaung' (valley), they divided into two groups. The leading section, which included Eric, advanced up the hill and came under a barrage of heavy fire. The second section moved round the valley to try to outflank the enemy. They had barely advanced twenty yards when they also came under heavy fire. In the heat of battle, Eric caught the full force of a grenade. He was struck down by several rounds of ammunition and fatally injured.

Major Lewton-Brain said in his letter that Eric had displayed bravery in combat and died gallantly doing his duty. He added by way of expiation that not a single Japanese had survived this action. He wrote that a whole company of British troops arrived quickly at the chaung and attacked the Japanese position from one side, while a Gurkha regiment attacked from the other. When these two companies united in combat, not a single live Japanese was left in the area: 28 enemy soldiers were counted dead at the end of the battle.

By the time Eric and his comrades in arms had passed through, British allies had recaptured Monywa and Mandalay from Japanese forces but, because of fierce battles taking place, it was not possible for him to make any inquiries about the whereabouts of mother.

Eric was killed on 29th May 1945 aged 23 years. His body was buried with due honours at Kanyunt Kwin Military Cemetery, near Toungoo, in central Burma. After the war, his body was re-buried with full military honours in the Military War Cemetery, Rangoon, where he lies to this day.

The 14th Army approached Rangoon at about the time the monsoon was expected to break, and it was a gamble as to which would arrive first, for the army's job would be considerably more difficult in a continuous downpour. However, a double assault by sea and air was put into operation, and the main forces closed in north of the river and landed just outside Rangoon. From there, they advanced on the city, amphibious forces making their first entry on 3rd May.

They had expected a concentration of Japanese to be defending the city and were fully prepared for a tough fight but, when the British forces landed, they found there was not a single Japanese left in the city. They had fled two days earlier, so Rangoon was quickly re-occupied without any encounter with the enemy. Allied forces released hundreds of prisoners of war and civilian internees, on the brink of starvation and disease, from the city jail. Like others, they told of the outrageous and inhumane treatment they had suffered at the hands of their Japanese captors.

Celebration

In June 1945, a great celebration took place in Rangoon. An Army and Air Force Victory Parade was held with great pomp and ceremony, followed by a stately Naval Review. The celebration was in honour of the men who had marched and fought for a thousand miles across some of the worst terrain in the world and had beaten the Japanese hands down. They had overcome the monsoon, malaria and other diseases. Now, in the words of Earl Mountbatten of Burma, "They had put on a splendid show"

Eric had missed the celebration by five weeks.

Eric

Eric was the tallest of my brothers; he was slim and kept himself fit and well. He had inherited father's light grey eyes that appeared to look into your very soul. He had dark brown hair and a light olive complexion. Walter said that, during his latter years after undergoing the rigorous training with the Chindits in Assam, he was in fine form and had developed a strong and muscular physique, often being mistaken for an American GI. But his accent distinguished him as a man born and bred in India. He was always cheerful and happy-go-lucky and, like Richard, was respected equally by his peers and working colleagues.

Aunty May conveyed the news about Eric on her next visit to us at school in Multan. Helen and I were greatly saddened when we heard the circumstances of his death and we went to the little Convent Chapel with the Mother Superior, our tears mingling with our prayers. We had lost not just our father but our beloved brother Eric as well.

So how could it be that the reports we read about daily, emanating from the battlefront, were so upbeat, declaring that the Allies were getting the upper hand in recapturing Burma; that they had reached Rangoon? And where was mother?

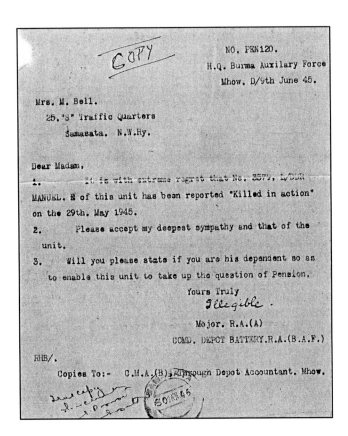

Above: A photocopy of the letter sent to Mrs Bell by the Burma Auxiliary Force to advise of Eric's death in action. The text reads: "Dear Madam, 1. It is with regret that No. 3579, L/BDR MANUEL. E of this unit has been reported 'Killed in action' on the 29th. May 1945. 2. Please accept my deepest sympathy and that of the unit. 3. Will you please state if you are his dependent so as to enable this unit to take up the question of Pension. Yours Truly (illegible signature) Mojor. R.A. (A) COMD. DEPOT BATTERY.R.A.(B.A.F.)" Presumably, 'Mojor' should have read 'Major'.

From.
Major D. Lewton-Braine.

No.3 Platoon,B.I.C.
Att.17 Ind.Div.SEAC
Dated the12th,June 1945

My dear Manuel,

    I am very sorry to have to break the news to you
that your brother Eric was killed in action on 29th,May 1945.
    What happened is this.A Burman came in to inform
the Company Commander with whom Eric was working,that there were
were Japs in the neighbourhood and volunteered to guide a part
to the spot.A Platoon was sent out with Eric accompanying them
to act as interpreterfor the guide.They came to a Chaung where
the enemy were located and the leading section advanced up it
only to come under heavy fire.The next section moved round to
try and out-flank the enemy,while Platoon HQ with whom your
brother was,followed the leading section up the Chaung.When
they had advanced about 20 yards they too came under heavy fire,
accompanied by grenades.Eric was struck by a grenade fragment
and fell,being struck simultaneously by several rounds.He was
killed outright.
    His body has been recovered and was buried in
KABYUNT-KWIN Military cemetary.The grave has been consecrated
by the R.C.Chaplain of the Division.
    Your brother died gallantly doing his duty as a
soldier and it may be some satisfaction to you to know that
NOT a single JAP survived the action.A whole company of British
Troops attacked the position from one side and Ghurkas from
the other when these two companies united up there was NOT a
live JAP in the area,28 dead bodies being counted.
    My chief regret is that Eric was not spared to
be re-united with his mother and you.I can only hope that you
menage to meet her soon.
    I have written to Mrs.Bell and sent a copy of
this letter to your other brother.

                           Yours sincerely,

Above: A photocopy of the letter sent to Eugene, which broke the news of Eric's death in action and provided a detailed account of the incident in which he was killed. The full text of the letter is reproduced overleaf, including the original formatting. As can be seen, the army typist went right up to the right hand edge of the page, and over it in places.

From:
    Major D. Lewton-Brain.

No.3 Platoon. B.I.C.
Att.17 Ind. Div. SEAC
Dated the 12th. June 1945

My dear Manuel.

I am very sorry to have to break the news to you that your brother Eric was killed in action on 29th. May 1945.

What happened is this. A Burman came in to inform the Company Commander with whom Eric was working, that that there were Japs in the neighbourhood and volunteered to guide a party to the spot. A Platoon was sent out with Eric accompanying them to act as interpreter for the guide. They came to a Chaung where the enemy were located and the leading section advanced up it only to come under heavy fire. The next section moved round to try to out-flank the enemy, while Platoon HQ with whom your brother was, followed the leading section up to the Chaung. When they had advanced about 20 yards they too came under heavy fire, accompanied by grenades. Eric was struck by a grenade fragment and fell, being struck simultaneously by several rounds. He was killed outright.

His body has been recovered and was buried in KANYUNT-KWIN Military cemetary (sic). The grave has been consecrated by the R.C. Chaplain of the Division.

Your brother died gallantly doing his duty as a soldier and it may be some satisfaction to you to know that NOT a single JAP survived the action. A whole company of British Troops attacked the position from one side and Ghurkas (sic) from the other. When these two companies united up there was NOT a live JAP in the area, 28 dead bodies being counted.

My chief regret is that Eric was not spared to be re-united with his mother and you. I can only hope that you manage to meet her soon.

I have written to Mrs. Bell and sent a copy of this letter to your other brother.

Yours sincerely.
D. Lewton-Brain (signature)

Above: The front of Eric's memorial card.

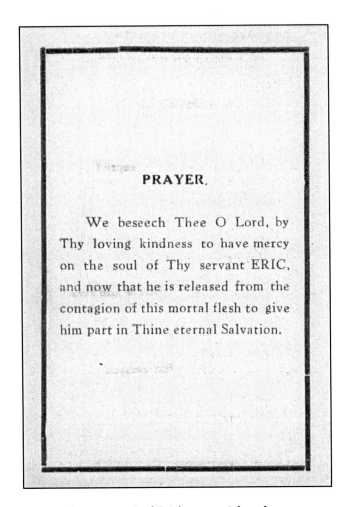

PRAYER.

We beseech Thee O Lord, by Thy loving kindness to have mercy on the soul of Thy servant ERIC, and now that he is released from the contagion of this mortal flesh to give him part in Thine eternal Salvation.

Above: Page 2 of Eric's memorial card.

REMEMBERANCE

No tomb Stones mark the sacred place
No pillars shew the grave
Of him, who died to free and make
This world a better state.

He is not here amongst us now
The dust has claimed its own
But while we live, and strive and vow
His name shall ne'er grow worn.

For he has fought and not in vain
Against great odds that seemed
                              too great
But now asleep and free from pain
He is our pride, our joy our own.

R. B.

Above: The final page of Eric's memorial card. As can be seen, this contains a poem by 'R.B.' – Ronnie Barnes, Eric's childhood friend from Lahore. To judge from the pasted alterations, it took Ronnie several attempts to get the words exactly as he wanted them.

Above:. Eugene in an undated photograph taken at Chaklala railway station.

Left: Tom and May Bell – Uncle Tom and Aunty May – at Peshawar, 1957; a time of relative stability after the upheavals of World War 2 and the Partition of India.

12

Walter Returns to Search for Mother

The Japanese had now been driven out of Burma, and Allied Forces were firmly in place in the capital, Rangoon.

At the cessation of hostilities, Walter was still with his unit in north-west Burma, from where he was ordered to report back to Imphal. From there, he was posted to Kalewa, Burma, and, within a few weeks of arriving, was discharged from the Royal Signals Corps. He decided to stay on in Kalewa in a civilian capacity and took up his old post of wireless operator in the Post & Telegraphs Department, where he had been employed before enlisting in the Chindits.

Kalewa is a small village surrounded by jungle and mountainous terrain, where living conditions and sanitation were very primitive. Within a few weeks of his arrival, Walter was struck down with a severe attack of dysentery and was told to report to the Post & Telegraphs office in Mandalay for treatment, and to take up his new post there.

When he passed through Mandalay, he was shocked to see the devastation and destruction of so many of the beautiful old Victorian buildings. Many of the ancient pagodas were shattered and burned beyond recognition. The imperial glory of the ancient palaces and gardens that had housed Burma's kings and queens before the British colonised the country were in ruins. Everywhere he looked, there were piles of rubble and debris with massive craters obstructing the straight that had once formed the beautiful tree-lined road he remembered so well. It was obvious that fierce battles had taken place here.

When Walter recovered from the shock of seeing such devastation, the first place he visited was the house that had been our home when we first arrived in Mandalay. It had even crossed his mind that, by some miracle, mother would be there. Of course, he realised he was deluding himself; it was just a dream. However, he was agreeably surprised to find that part of the building that was formerly our home and father's office was still standing, although much damage had been done to the rear. The servants' quarters were a pile of rubble. What had been a beautifully kept garden was now a pitted, churned-up field. Walter later discovered that the Japanese had used this house as their headquarters right up to the time the Allied forces had driven them out. There was evidence that, days before they fled, the Japanese had torched the building, in much the same way as the Allied forces had done when the Japanese were expected to invade. What had once been a beautifully polished floor was now blackened and charred, and almost turned to coal.

Walter, with the help of a government grant, set

about repairing the building in an attempt to put it to its original use – that of the main office of the Post & Telegraphs Department. He could not believe the strange coincidence that he was now working in the same office that father had occupied, and which had been our home for a short time before he was transferred to Monywa.

Walter felt confident that he was now in a better location to find out the whereabouts of mother. He set about making enquiries at various government departments and information centres, trying to contact people who might have some knowledge of what happened to sick, elderly or infirm people during the Japanese occupation. After numerous enquiries, Walter was told of a man by the name of Rashid who had remained in the area throughout the war and had a sound local knowledge of what had taken place and who might give him a lead.

Rashid was indeed happy to help Walter, and they decided to start the search at a place where mother and father were last known to have stayed. The following day, Walter and Rashid took the only local transport, a broken-down bus overloaded and overburdened with humanity, to Monywa. Again, when they arrived, they witnessed scenes of terrible devastation. Not a single building was recognisable. Many had been burned to the ground. Some effort was being made to clear up the debris, but the foul smell of smouldering rubbish and dead animals still hung in the oppressively hot air.

Water and Rashid made numerous enquiries of local authorities and asked local people, but could get no definite information about the vital few weeks before the Japanese forces had invaded the area.

Finally, after three days of searching and questioning, through some local Burmese people who had worked for father at the Post & Telegraphs Department, they had a lucky break. They were able to track down Raj Gopal – a man who had previously been employed as our gardener.

13

Mappoo's Story

Raj knew all about mother and father and remembered the day father took us to join the convoy of evacuees leaving Monywa. He recalled the days that followed and mother's distress after we had left. He was there when the bombs fell and they all had to run to the shelter. He recalled how scared they all were, how mother kept calling our names and how father had tried to calm and reassure her.

Raj said that father had found a local woman by the name of Mappoo, a former Burmese teacher, whom he appointed to take care of mother. He told of the important role Mappoo had played in the care and welfare of mother in the dark days of Japanese occupation. He said Mappoo lived in the village; he would find out exactly where and be happy to accompany Walter and Rashid to her home. Raj said that Mappoo was now in a poor state of health, but her memory of those traumatic years remained undiminished. She would be able to tell him of mother's final journey.

On the appointed day, Walter and Rashid followed Raj through a maze of little streets to the home of Mappoo, a small woman with white hair and a dark wrinkled face. Her fingers were crippled with arthritis. And, as they all sat on the floor of Mappoo's tiny room drinking tea, the sad story came tumbling out. She spoke quietly and simply, frequently wiping her tears with the corner of her tunic as she related what had happened after we left home.

Mappoo spoke of how father had employed her, how he instructed her to take personal care of mother, never to leave her side. She remembered mother being confined to bed most of the time, unable to do much for herself. She had to cook and feed mother. She would massage her feet and back and generally tend to her needs. She said mother got increasingly confused in mind and low in spirit. It caused father a great deal of worry when he had to leave her, sometimes for up to a week, to carry out work up country. She could not be left alone.

Mappoo and Raj said that, about two weeks after we left Monywa, the air attacks started in earnest. "Nobody seemed to know what to do or how to escape the bombs that kept falling from the sky. There was panic in the streets with people rushing around searching for cover. Every corner you turned was strewn with debris caused by houses collapsing into the street. There was no one left in charge, no one they could turn to for help. The people in authority had themselves fled. The whole situation deteriorated rapidly, with law and order breaking down completely. Youths began looting shops, and young children, apparently abandoned, were left screaming in the streets, some from wounds they had sustained from flying debris, others with serious burns and broken limbs. It was terrible; so many injured, nobody to help. There was no one they could turn to for help," she repeated, her tears flowing freely.

Because father could not quit his job by simply walking away, he had to stay to the end and make the decision finally for mother to leave. He instructed Mappoo to accompany her on the ferry expected to leave the next day. He also instructed Raj Gopal to accompany them. There was no time to lose, they had to leave early in the morning, he would follow as soon as he could, very possibly the day after, he said reassuringly.

They joined a party of about twelve people aboard one of the few remaining boats by the riverside. After a quick exchange of promises between mother and father to meet the following day, they boarded the boat which was pushed off by men using long poles, as they could not start up the engine.

The rains had swollen the river and they were travelling upstream against a fast current. They were two days into their journey when they began to be strafed by low-flying enemy aircraft. They tried to take cover close to the riverbank under the overhanging trees, but it proved to be poor protection, for Japanese foot soldiers appeared on the bank through the trees, attracted by the noisy spluttering of the engine. There were not many, just three or four heavily armed men. They began shouting, gesturing with their guns, ordering them to turn back. Here now was the barbarian race from the Land of the Rising Sun causing terror among this small group of people.

All the while, Mappoo and Raj Gopal stayed close to mother who, by this time, was in deep shock, unable to walk through the tangles up the steep bank without their help. Raj Gopal was able to improvise a rough seat made of broken bits of bamboo, tied together with vines, in which they sat mother and carried her slowly the short distance back to Monywa. This act of kindness could only be attributed to the loyalty and allegiance they felt towards mother and father.

During the walk, this small group of twelve were constantly prodded with rifle butts and shouted at in foul and guttural language ordering them to keep a steady pace. It is well known how inhumane the actions of the Japanese were, how terrible their crimes, how they terrorised innocent people. It can only be imagined what terror my mother, Mappoo and Raj Gopal and their little group experienced during this short walk. Most of them had not eaten for days, for their captors provided no food or water. No one could tell how many atrocities were committed, nor how many innocent lives were lost during this time.

When they arrived back at Monywa, bruised and battered, hungry, thirsty and tired, they were told by their captors to return to their homes. Mother, Mappoo and Raj Gopal arrived back at our home. They had been away for five days. They had expected to see a few familiar faces. Father had employed linesmen, coolies and domestic staff numbering 50 or more. But mother returned home to find the house deserted. Neither father, staff nor servants were anywhere to be seen.

It was Mappoo who suggested that they take mother

to Mandalay. She knew Father Mainier, who ran a Catholic mission there; she knew well the school run by nuns. He might be able to help them. It was Mappoo who persuaded mother to let them try to get a place there. Mappoo was certain the nuns, if they were still there, would accept them. If they were accepted, mother would be safe in the care of the Sisters of Charity. Mappoo herself, she argued, was also in need of a refuge. Raj Gopal would attempt to get some form of transport, a bullock cart perhaps, to convey them.

Mother did not know where father was at this point. He had told her he would catch up with her the following day, so she expected him back at any moment. Obviously neither mother, Mappoo nor Raj were aware that father had left and was already on his way to India.

At first, mother was not in favour of Mappoo's suggestion at leaving Monywa without informing father. She said they should wait just one more day; father will definitely turn up. But as time went on, mother was less able to make decisions for herself. "Every day she grew weaker, physically and mentally," Mapoo said, between sobs. Eventually, after three days, mother agreed to be taken to Mandalay. Struggling on in Monywa, without proper food, water or protection from looters, was proving impossible. They were now all in agreement that the move to Mandalay was their only hope of getting help. After days of persistent pleadings against the restrictions of the capricious Japanese Commandant, Raj Gopal finally obtained permission for them to leave.

For the next three or four days, they travelled in a

bullock cart on the bumpy pot-holed road to Mandalay. Then they arrived, at last, at the Church of the Sacred Heart and were received by the Parish Priest, Father Mainier, with compassion and sympathy. The kindly priest had spent almost a lifetime working and preaching in Burma since arriving from his native France. He listened in silence to Mappoo, whom he remembered well; she had taught in his school many years before. She told him of the rigours and trials of their journey since leaving Monywa, explaining that she had promised my father to take care of mother. "Our house is no longer safe and we have nowhere to go. It was my suggestion that we come here. Now Mrs Manuel is desperately in need of care. She is very tired."

Mother was incoherent by this time. She had not eaten for several days and was reduced to a skeleton. Her heels were sore and very painful. She kept calling my father's name, saying, "My husband will be here very soon to take me home. The children are waiting for me. I have to go to them."

Father Mainier tried to comfort mother saying, "The nuns will take good care of you until your husband arrives to fetch you, Mrs Manuel. Try not to worry." He accompanied her and Mappoo, still in the bullock cart, down the road a short distance to the next compound. They came to a high brick wall surrounding a large building and, when Father Mainier unlocked the large iron gates, she noticed the little wooden plaque fixed to the pillar of the entrance. It read: 'St. Joseph's Orphanage'.

The gardens inside looked untouched by the chaos

and destruction outside; there were beds of flowering bushes and the lawn was neatly trimmed. They passed a grotto that housed a statue of the Virgin Mary that had survived the bombing raids, but further along the drive there was a crater where a large tree had been uprooted, lying on its side. There were signs of damage to one corner of the building that appeared to have taken a direct hit. It was covered with a dark green tarpaulin.

Mother Superior Gabriel greeted them warmly in her little office next to the Chapel. She was a large buxom woman from Belgium. In days gone by, she had a round jolly face and kind, smiling eyes. Now she bore a sad countenance and her smile was somewhat constrained. She was moved to tears when Father Mainier told her of mother's plight. She assured mother that she would find a safe haven here. "We are very busy at the moment, our home is quite full, but we will find you a nice room, Mrs Manuel, and Mappoo can stay to look after you. But first of all, we will get you both something to eat, then clean and dress your feet. You will feel better after a rest."

It was time for mother to say goodbye to Raj Gopal, who had stayed constantly by her side during these past few arduous weeks against all the odds. In spite of her discomfort and mental anguish, mother was very aware that Raj had been her mainstay. It was he and Mappoo who had now brought her to this place of safety. She shook his hand appreciatively and said, "This is not goodbye, Raj. When my husband returns, we will take you back with us to Monywa. Thank you for all you have done for me."

Mappoo continued to tell Walter her story, her eyes brimming over with tears, her heart full, finding it almost impossible to relate the pain and suffering of the last few years she had shared in mother's life. "Your mother," Mappoo said between sobs, "could not take in any of the things that were happening to her when she first entered the doors of the orphanage." There was nothing in this small, sparsely furnished room to remind her of her past life, her ordered home or her family. How did she come to be in this strange place?

"Where's my husband?" mother kept repeating. "Where are the children?" No one could tell her. No one could reassure her. She retreated into depths of anguish and despair; her mind was giving up, she was no longer aware of her surroundings or how she came to be in this place. She was deranged almost. She was still expecting father to come through the door at any moment to take her home. Why was he so long in coming? She kept calling his name. "Eugene, dear. I'm in here. Where are you? Where are the children?"

She continued to cry out repeatedly throughout the day, calling for each of us in turn. "Helen, my baby", "Maude, my child", "Blanche, my lovely", "Richard," "Walter, Eric, Eugene, where are you all?"

Outside the walls of the convent, the Japanese wielded complete control, but thank God they left this little community alone. However, food was becoming scarce and what little vegetables the nuns and workers were able to grow were quickly consumed, for there were many hungry mouths to feed. Orphaned children were brought in every day. The nuns had little money to buy food in the thriving black market. Within the high walls, many members of this small community were falling ill through malnutrition and lack of medicine.

The cracked, dry skin around mother's heels was not healing; they were now painful, open sores. She could barely walk. She depended more and more on Mappoo to wash and dress her feet, to relieve her pain and bring her a little rice and lentil soup each day. Mother Gabriel and Father Mainier came to her room often to try to comfort and calm her frenzied mind. They were upset and grieved that they were unable to provide her with proper nourishment and medical care. These days, they were heavy-hearted at seeing the plight of so many of their charges facing a similar situation. Towards them all they felt a great sense of helplessness.

The hot summer of 1944 passed slowly and there was no relief for members of the convent by way of food or medicine. The nuns and carers themselves were falling ill. Malaria and smallpox were the worst killers. There were also outbreaks of typhus and polio but, because these cases were detected early, they were isolated and, to some extent, contained. But there were many whose immune systems were too weak to resist these diseases who succumbed.

Mappoo continued the story amid sobs, saying that a piece of land near the convent had been set aside for a burial ground, and after prayers each day the deceased were wrapped in cotton sheets and placed in shallow graves. Almost every morning, there was someone waiting to be buried.

On 7th November 1944, four months before British forces recaptured Mandalay, mother passed away, aged 44 years. No stone or cross marks her final place of rest.

14

Multan

It was mid September 1946. I was sixteen and Helen ten. We had settled into our daily routine as boarders in St. Mary's Convent in Multan. Aunty May and Uncle Tom would visit us some weekends, and accompany us back to Samasata for Easter and Christmas and the three-month summer holiday. During his annual leave, Eugene would also visit us regularly with little treats of sweets and nuts.

Naturally we spoke often of mother. It seemed all we could do was pray that she was still safe. Until we could do something positive and practical, all we could do was hope. Hope was the key that kept us from going crazy with worry. We faced each day with hope in our hearts. Hope that the postman would bring news from her, hope that we would receive official notification of her whereabouts, hope that she was well. Please God, let her join us here, soon.

On one particular day, Helen and I were called to Reverend

Mother's office. We thought it odd to be called away from our morning lessons. We were full of foreboding; we must have done something bad. What was it? But when we walked into the office, we were taken aback to see at Aunty and Uncle sitting there quietly, looking anxious and ill at ease. "What's the matter, Aunty? Is there something wrong?" we asked.

Aunty May was the first to answer, rather hesitantly. She had trouble finding the right words. What she tried to say choked in her throat. Tears began trickling down her face. Her mouth was quivering and her words broke into pieces. But it was not difficult to work out what she was trying to say. "Walter has discovered some very sad news," she said. "He has learnt what happened to mother. I am so sorry ... but your dear mother passed away two years ago."

Silence. Blank thoughts. What did you say? Are you sure? Is Walter sure?

I could hear Aunty speaking softly, something about her being cared for right to the end. But I could not take it in. I was staring at the little statue of Our Lady in the corner of the room. I could vaguely hear Mother Antoine saying that mother was with the Lord. She was free from pain and suffering. Her passing was a blessed release. Helen was crying noisily. But I did not cry. I was looking around the room full of religious images, my mind a blank.

Mother Antoine stood up and walked round the table. She put her arms around Helen and me and led us towards the chapel with Aunty and Uncle following. I seemed to float slowly down the corridor, not able to take in the full meaning of what had been said. I could hear her saying some prayers but was empty, devoid of feeling.

Afterwards, we were invited into the parlour and served cups of tea and biscuits. Aunty then told us of mother's last days. The pain she must have suffered and the mental anguish, never knowing we were safe and well.

Right up to this time, we had prayed that mother would be in a safe place, believing that one day we would be reunited with her. We had never given up hope. Now she was gone.

The war was officially over at last – after all these years. We had made it safely through but, to our great sorrow, our beloved mother, father and brother had not, nor did they know that we were safe and well and would go on to live happy, fruitful and successful lives in Australia, Canada and England.

Right: An undated photograph of Blanche, probably taken in the late 1940s or early 1950s.

Left: Maude, photographed in Lahore on 21st October 1949.

Epilogue

India in Turmoil, 1947

Muslim, Hindu and Sikh communities had lived side by side in harmony for hundreds of years. Now divisions between the various religious factions had started to manifest themselves in many ways. Mobs staged numerous noisy demonstrations throughout the sub-continent. Banner-bearing fanatics were demanding that the British quit India. Every day, there were incidents of anarchy and rioting in the streets, burning and looting in the bazaars. There were many murders among neighbours who, up to now, had lived together in peace and harmony.

The throwing of stones by children into homes occupied by British and European families was becoming a common occurrence. Insolent Indians jeered at members of the families of British and Eurasians, demonstrating their contempt by spitting on the ground as they passed them in the street.

The newspapers were replete with reports of meetings between the ruling British government, the Congress party and other political factions. There were Hindu demands, Muslim demands, Sikh demands.

Mahatma Gandhi was calling for the immediate independence of India, touring the country and preaching to small groups in back yards about his policy of non-cooperation and non-violence. Gatherings of people in this volatile climate, when whipped up by inflammatory speeches by an agitator, inevitably lead to violence. The Muslim League under Mohammed Ali Jinnah demanded a separate nation for the Muslim minority. Each section of India seemed to be demanding independence for their own party or religious group.

There was talk of the division of India into two and then three different sectors. India would consist of the main mass of land in the middle. East Pakistan would cover Assam and the fertile delta area of the river Ganges. West Pakistan would consist of the Punjab, the Indus valley and part of Kashmir in the north-west, down to the port of Karachi on the edge of the Arabian Gulf. There were even discussions of a corridor linking East and West Pakistan. Speculation and uncertainty were rife.

At this time, it was obligatory for all employees in the armed services – the Army, Navy and Air Force as well as the civil government – to relinquish their commitment to the British government. In late 1946, Eugene was required to transfer from the British Army and opt for service under the Union of India. He was seconded to the Indian Army and stationed at Jubbulpur. He realised that, if the stories circulating in the press were to be believed and the division of India was to take place, Helen and I in Multan, with its Muslim majority, were likely to be cut off in territory forming part of the new state of West Pakistan. As he was now in the Indian Army, he might be restricted or even forbidden from visiting us in Pakistan. At this point, no one knew exactly where the borders between the two new states, India and Pakistan, were to be drawn.

Eugene therefore reckoned it would be best for Helen to be in India. She was young, just ten years old; he was her official guardian and she would need his financial support for a few years to come. I was now in the final months of schooling and due to sit my matriculation examination, so he felt confident that I was old enough to make my own decision about my future.

Eugene's next task was to set about finding a boarding school for Helen in that sector of the country that was more likely to remain in India after the impending partition. In this, he was lucky for he discovered that Reverend Mother Antoine had recently been transferred from Multan to Dalhousie, a beautiful area located in the foothills of the Himalayas. It enjoyed a temperate climate and was well known to be a haven of cool during the hot weather, where many families from the hot plains spent the summer months. Eugene had had a good relationship with Mother Antoine during the time that Helen and I had been at St. Mary's Convent in Multan, so when he applied for Helen to be admitted to the Dalhousie Convent she was happy to accept her. It turned out to be a fortuitous move for Eugene, for with some encouragement from Mother Antoine he met Sheila Godfrey, a teacher at the convent whom he was later to marry.

Aunty May and Uncle Tom accompanied Helen to her new school at Dalhousie, where they met up with

Eugene and placed her in the care and guidance of our family friend and benefactor – Mother Antoine.

Independence Day, 15th August 1947

India celebrated Independence Day on 15th August 1947. After months of speculation, the division of India into three separate states turned out to be the only solution to satisfy the two majority groups: Muslim and Hindu. The Hindu majority in central and southern India became the Union of India, while the two smaller land areas on either side of it, and composed of a Muslim majority, were to be called West and East Pakistan.

The birth of these new nations was painful in the extreme and costly in terms of human lives, for thousands of Hindus living in the newly formed state of Pakistan found themselves on wrong side of the border, as did Muslims living in India. Ancient divisions and prejudices began to manifest themselves. Muslims would not be allowed into the kitchens of Hindus, nor were they permitted to drink from the same tap. People were being discriminated against, abused and, in many instances, killed by their counterparts. It seemed that the authorities had made little or no effort for a smooth changeover ahead of the final division of India; there was no overall plan or proper guidance from those in authority.

Many people had no alternative but to flee to the side decreed by political rulers to become their future homeland.

Hoards of people were uprooted. Seventy million people found themselves on the wrong side of the dividing line and were fleeing across the borders in both directions to escape bloody riots taking place between sectarian groups. The border between India and its new neighbour, Pakistan, became a river of blood as the exodus erupted into rioting at every border crossing. People huddled together on to bullock carts or horse-drawn vehicles, tongas, cycles, trains or on foot, trying to drive their livestock on unmade tracks to get to the other side. Many women were carrying their children on their hips and their belongings on their heads. There were some women who gave birth by the wayside, so weak they could no longer carry them, having to abandon their newborn in the dust and heat. There was no food or water. After two or three days, their numbers grew less.

Every railway station was crowded with desperate families, some lying unattended for days, dressed in rags, weary and starving, waiting to board trains to take them across borders. Nor was it safe to travel by train. Every train leaving the numerous stations throughout the sub-continent was crowded to its fullest capacity. Railway carriages were full of women and children, while the men jostled and squeezed on to running boards and hung on to handrails. Desperate people packed themselves into every available space on the roofs of trains and even sat on the buffers. In whichever way they could, they travelled towards the border. But all too often, as the train came within sight of the official border, it was forced to stop by cows led on to the line by the opposing party, with armed gangs laying in wait. Thousands of men, women and children – both Muslim and Hindu – were mercilessly slaughtered in cold blood. The massive exchange of population that took place was unprecedented. It was horrendous. It left behind death and destruction at nearly every border crossing throughout the country.

The migration was a massive exercise in human misery. The Partition of India ranks, beyond a doubt, as one of the greatest tragedies in human history.

Aunty May and Uncle Tom were well aware of what was happening and extremely concerned about the welfare of staff and servants who had to leave suddenly at short notice because no one seemed to know where the border line was to be drawn. When it was eventually decided that their district was to become West Pakistan, the railway station at Samasata quickly became crowded with Hindu families waiting to board the trains to travel to what was to become India.

Tom was one of many able to befriend his Hindu colleagues, who hid friends in places they knew to be safe before helping them across the border, knowing they would sometimes have to walk miles through the arid and inhospitable desert.

One evening as it was getting dusk, Tom spotted a man, cowed and frightened, whom he judged from the clothes he was wearing to be a Hindu, taking shelter under a tree near the house. Tom invited him in and, after a meal and a wash, sent him off with a tiffin carrier containing food and a bottle of water sufficient to last him for a few days. We never did discover if he reached safety, or what became of the family he may have left behind.

The dreadful events taking place all over the country as a result of the Partition did not directly affect our community in Samasata. Being Christian and neutral in the conflict between Muslim and Hindu, our lives continued comparatively normally, though we were sometimes caught up in the bloodshed. Very much later I learnt from Ivor, who was to become my husband, that, while travelling by rail from Quetta to Lahore with his parents, the train was stopped in a remote area. Armed men boarded and killed several Hindus in cold blood. He said he would never forget the Muslim attackers – they looked crazy and wild with rage in their determination to kill. For many years, Ivor was traumatised by what he witnessed that day and could not or would not speak of the horrors of that journey. All he did say was that he and his parents were terrified and were lucky to have escaped with their lives.

Late August 1947

Our family had now become separated by the Partition of India; borders were closed. Helen was in Dalhousie, India; Eugene in Jubbulpur, India; Walter in Calcutta, India.; Richard in Tel Aviv, Palestine; and Blanche in Quetta, West Pakistan. I was in the convent at Multan in West Pakistan, while Aunty May and Uncle Tom remained in Samasata, West Pakistan. From here, all our lives were destined to go in different directions.

Fifty years were to pass before I saw Eugene, Walter or Helen again.

Eugene remained in the Indian Army until he retired in 1970. He had been on various postings all over India, including Jammu, Jhansi, Sholapur, Kirkee, Poona and Ferozapore. On retirement, he decided to settle in Bangalore. Eugene and his wife, Sheila, who taught at the local school, lived busy lives, devoting all their energy to giving their six children a good education. They succeeded in achieving qualifications that enabled them to secure good jobs in India. Eugene's son, Philip, was the first member of his family to migrate to Australia in 1983 and, over the space of a few years, he was able to help other family members to follow him towards a better life. All the family have since settled happily in the outskirts of Melbourne.

Walter returned to Burma after the war and was reinstated in a civilian capacity in the Telegraph Department in Mandalay, in his original place of employment. By coincidence, he worked in the building where my father had once worked as head of department. While he was in Mandalay, he married a Burmese girl, Regina, in 1950. They had three children, Noel, Lena and Patsy. After Burma was given independence from Britain in 1948, all groups of ethnic standing had to legally declare their allegiance to the new state. Walter was then officially registered as a citizen of Burma. However, a few months later, the Government of Burma ordered those who were not of Burmese descent to quit the country. In 1973, therefore, Walter and his young family migrated to Perth, Western Australia.

Eric was killed in action on 29th May 1945 in Toungoo, Burma, aged 22 years. Today his name is commemorated in the Register of the Commonwealth War Graves Commission in Rangoon.

Richard enlisted in the British Army in 1942. He married Florise (from Mauritius) in a simple ceremony in Tel Aviv. He was awarded several medals: the Africa Star, the Defence Medal, the War Medal 1939-1945 and the General Service Medal with clasp, Palestine, 1945-1948.

Richard was a quiet, unassuming man who seldom spoke of his experiences during the time he served in the Royal Army Ordnance Corps. He seemed to take all hardships in his stride, just as he had done during our trek through the jungle, and was able to shake off setbacks and difficulties without much damage to his sunny disposition. He was a jolly person, happy-go-lucky in company, always popular with his colleagues, laughing with great gusto and enjoying the yarns they spun. Certainly he was fun-loving and carefree, and had shaken off the difficult, violent years of his childhood.

He returned to Karachi and was discharged from the Army in 1949. Florise and their daughter, Teresa (born in 1947), had joined Richard in Karachi 1948, but Florise was not happy and their marriage failed. Florise and Teresa returned to their homeland, Mauritius, and unfortunately lost touch with Richard. He then had a relationship with Hilda, with whom he had a daughter, Charmaine. Quite suddenly one day, without any explanation, Hilda walked out on them both. Richard was left shocked and bewildered at her sudden departure, but cared and nurtured Charmaine throughout her young life. Charmaine's marriage to Freddy was a great delight, for he was very proud of her.

Richard held a responsible job with the General Motors Corporation of the USA in Karachi for many years. He joined a strike with other workers for better working conditions but was immediately dismissed for having taken part. Workers in Pakistan do not have the right of appeal, whatever the circumstances, especially against large companies such as General Motors. This blighted Richard's job prospects with other companies.

Sadly for Richard and all the family, after a few years his life took a downturn. He took on odd jobs while looking after his daughter, Charmaine, but his health was failing and he suffered severe attacks of asthma. He died in Karachi in lamentable conditions in 1986, aged 62.

Richard mellowed in later life, spending much of his time with Blanche's children, teaching them the skills that he had later learned in woodwork and joinery, always answering their questions and patiently pointing out the different types of wood and how they were best suited to particular pieces of furniture. He retained strong links with all the family and, if any of us were in trouble or needed help, he was always first on the scene, always ready to help. He gave his all. Whatever he possessed he gave to others, keeping for himself only sufficient for his basic needs. As Richard grew older, he grew generous to the point that one felt he was neglecting himself.

Blanche joined the Women's Auxiliary Corps in 1943 as a telephone operator and later as a secretary in GEC, a private engineering company where she met Pete D'Souza. They married and had four children. They lived in Karachi, always trying to help Richard during his lean years. During this time, Richard taught Blanche's children all he knew of carpentry and cabinet-making, from which they now earn their living. Blanche and her young family of four, Cora, Robert, Colin and Stephen, migrated to Perth, Western Australia, in October 1975.

After completing her schooling, Helen lived with Eugene and his family, helping in bringing up his children. She accompanied Eugene's family on their numerous postings, one of them being to Panagar, 90 miles north of Calcutta. It was there that she met her future husband, Edwin, whom she married and by whom she had four children. They lived in a small apartment in Calcutta with Edwin's mother, in extremely cramped conditions. Edwin worked hard but the family struggled for many years. When Helen's eldest daughter, Heather, was working as a receptionist in a large hotel in Calcutta, she met a Canadian, Edmund, whom she married before migrating to Canada. Within a few months, she was able to obtain permission for her family in Calcutta to migrate to Scarborough, Canada, in 1988, where they now reside.

Aunty May and Uncle Tom, who had played a pivotal role in our lives, did not have children of their own. Uncle Tom died in Lahore, after which Aunty May migrated to Perth, Australia, in 1980. She lived with her sister, Enid, until she qualified for an apartment of her own when she took on the role of matriarch to the now extended family. She was very much loved by all. When she died in 1989 at the age of 83, she was given a large funeral.

Maude. At the end of my education, I worked as a secretary in Lahore where I met and married Ivor Hitchcock, whose parents had returned to England in May 1953 to live in Hythe, Southampton. Ivor and I migrated to Britain in 1953 to join them. Ivor was called up for National Service in 1958 and remained in the RAF for 24 years, during which time we had the opportunity to travel to several places around the

UK and abroad, including Germany and Aden. We had three children, Rita, Christine and Martyn. Sadly, in 1994 my family and I were devastated when Ivor suddenly suffered a heart attack and passed away, aged 64.

I later married Albert Kilvington, to whom I owe a huge debt of gratitude for giving me the opportunity to travel and meet up again with my brothers and sisters in Australia and Canada – and, in spite of their protestations, persuading them to recall their experiences, and supporting me throughout in my effort to piece together and record some of the events that took place during those fateful years.

Glossary

Terms not explained in the text

ayah, n. Native Indian nurse or lady's maid.

brinjal, n. Aubergine or egg-plant.

brinjal bhurta, n. Dish of aubergines with spices.

burfie, n. Indian dessert made from coconut.

chappaties, n. Indian flatbread.

charpoy, n. The word means literally 'four legs' and refers to the Indian daybed that is widely used throughout the country; as a stringed bed to sleep on, or a daybed for ladies to lounge on and conduct their daily affairs.

coir, n. Fibres found between the husk and outer shell of a coconut

coolie, n. Manual labourer from Asia, particularly China and India.

dacoits, n. Armed robbers/bandits working in gangs.

dah, n. Type of knife used in Burma.

dhal, n. The Indian word for lentils.

gullab jamon, n. Dessert made from dough consisting mainly of milk solids (often including double cream and flour) in a sugar syrup flavoured with cardamom seeds and rosewater or saffron.

gully-dunda, n. A sort of bat-and-ball game played with a 3 ft. long stick and a 4 in. piece of wood. The piece of wood is hit with the stick so that it jumps into the air and is then batted as far as possible.

hulwa, n. Sweet confection of sugar, honey, fruit, egg white, sesame seeds or nuts formed into balls or logs.

kukri, n. Curved knife originating from Nepal, used as both a tool and weapon.

lungi, n. Long piece of brightly coloured cloth (cotton or silk) used as clothing (a skirt or loincloth or sash etc.) in Burma, India and Pakistan.

marlies, n. Gardeners.

pice, n., pl. The rupee is subdivided into one hundred paise (singular paisa) or pice.

pillau, n. Oriental dish of rice with meat, spices, etc.

punkah, n. A type of fan; originally a portable fan made from the leaf of the palmyra.

rattan, n. Tropical climbing plant with thin, tough stems.

telegraphist, n. An operator who uses morse code to communicate by land or radio lines.

tiffin, n. The term 'tiffin' refers to the Indian-English custom of enjoying a light lunch or snack between meals. It was such a popular custom that a special lunchbox was designed to carry the lunch, e.g. to work.

tonga, n.. Light two-wheeled vehicle used in India.

wallah, n. Person or thing employed for a particular purpose, e.g. tonga-wallah.